Fresh Anointing

Kenneth E. Hagin

Unless otherwise indicated, all Scripture quotations in this volume are from the *King James Version* of the Bible.

Sixth Printing 1995

ISBN 0-89276-514-3

In the U.S. write:
Kenneth Hagin Ministries
P.O. Box 50126
Tulsa, OK 74150-0126

In Canada write:
Kenneth Hagin Ministries
P.O. Box 335, Station D,
Etobicoke (Toronto), Ontario
Canada, M9A 4X3

BOOKS BY KENNETH E. HAGIN

* Redeemed From Poverty, Sickness and Spiritual Death
* What Faith Is
* Seven Vital Steps To Receiving the Holy Spirit
* Right and Wrong Thinking
  Prayer Secrets
* Authority of the Believer (foreign only)
* How To Turn Your Faith Loose
  The Key to Scriptural Healing
  Praying To Get Results
  The Present-Day Ministry of Jesus Christ
  The Gift of Prophecy
  Healing Belongs to Us
  The Real Faith
  How You Can Know the Will of God
  Man on Three Dimensions
  The Human Spirit
  Turning Hopeless Situations Around
  Casting Your Cares Upon the Lord
  Seven Steps for Judging Prophecy
* The Interceding Christian
  Faith Food for Autumn
* Faith Food for Winter
  Faith Food for Spring
  Faith Food for Summer
* New Thresholds of Faith
* Prevailing Prayer to Peace
* Concerning Spiritual Gifts
  Bible Faith Study Course
  Bible Prayer Study Course
  The Holy Spirit and His Gifts
* The Ministry Gifts (Study Guide)
  Seven Things You Should Know About Divine Healing
  El Shaddai
  Zoe: The God-Kind of Life
  A Commonsense Guide to Fasting
  Must Christians Suffer?
  The Woman Question
  The Believer's Authority
  Ministering to Your Family
  What To Do When Faith Seems Weak and Victory Lost
  Growing Up, Spiritually
  Bodily Healing and the Atonement (Dr. T.J. McCrossan)
  Exceedingly Growing Faith
  Understanding the Anointing
  I Believe in Visions
  Understanding How To Fight the Good Fight of Faith
  Plans, Purposes, and Pursuits
  How You Can Be Led by the Spirit of God
  A Fresh Anointing
  Classic Sermons
  He Gave Gifts Unto Men:
      A Biblical Perspective of Apostles, Prophets, and Pastors
  The Art of Prayer

Following God's Plan For Your Life
The Triumphant Church: Dominion Over All the Powers of Darkness
Healing Scriptures
Mountain-Moving Faith
Love: The Way to Victory
Biblical Keys to Financial Prosperity
The Price Is Not Greater Than God's Grace (Mrs. Oretha Hagin)

MINIBOOKS (A partial listing)

* *The New Birth*
* *Why Tongues?*
* *In Him*
* *God's Medicine*
* *You Can Have What You Say*
* *Don't Blame God*
* *Words*
  Plead Your Case
* *How To Keep Your Healing*
  The Bible Way To Receive the Holy Spirit
  I Went to Hell
  How To Walk in Love
  The Precious Blood of Jesus
* *Love Never Fails*
  How God Taught Me About Prosperity

BOOKS BY KENNETH HAGIN JR.

* *Man's Impossibility — God's Possibility*
  Because of Jesus
  How To Make the Dream God Gave You Come True
  Forget Not!
  God's Irresistible Word
  Healing: Forever Settled
  Don't Quit! Your Faith Will See You Through
  The Untapped Power in Praise
  Listen to Your Heart
  What Comes After Faith?
  Speak to Your Mountain!
  Come Out of the Valley!
  It's Your Move!
  God's Victory Plan

MINIBOOKS (A partial listing)

* *Faith Worketh by Love*
* *Seven Hindrances to Healing*
* *The Past Tense of God's Word*
  Faith Takes Back What the Devil's Stolen
  How To Be a Success in Life
  Get Acquainted With God
  Unforgiveness
  Ministering to the Brokenhearted

*These titles are also available in Spanish. Information about other foreign translations of several of the above titles (i.e., Finnish, French, German, Indonesian, Polish, Russian, etc.) may be obtained by writing to: Kenneth Hagin Ministries, P.O. Box 50126, Tulsa, Oklahoma 74150-0126.

Contents

Preface

There is nothing so important in this hour as for the Body of Christ to be full of the Word of God and full of the Spirit of God. The time has long since passed for following man-made plans and formulas. We need the Word of God in our hearts and the anointing of God upon our lives so we can prosper in everything we do. We need to stay in God's Presence and find out what the Head of the Church, the Lord Jesus Christ, has in mind, and then be sure to do it. God has not hidden from His people what He wants to do; it's all laid out in the New Testament. And it is only by following God's New Testament plan and being filled up to overflowing with God's Spirit that we will be equipped to participate in the revival in these last days and to bring Jesus the glory and honor due His Name. Also, if we follow God's New Testament plan for the Church, every believer will be able to take his place and fulfill his function in the Body of Christ. However, in order for believers to be able to do this, it is crucial that each one of us experience *a fresh anointing*. We are to be continually filled with God's Spirit so that we can be used by God mightily in these days to fulfill His will in our lives. God has made an abundant provision for His people to be filled up at all times with His Spirit, regardless of outward circumstances, so we can live unto His glory!

Chapter 1
The Anointing in the Old Testament

It is a good thing to give thanks unto the Lord, and to sing praises unto thy name, O most High:

To shew forth thy lovingkindness in the morning, and thy faithfulness every night,

Upon an instrument of ten strings, and upon the psaltery; upon the harp with a solemn sound.

For thou, Lord, hast made me glad through thy work: I will triumph in the works of thy hands.

O Lord, how great are thy works! and thy thoughts are very deep.

A brutish man knoweth not; neither doth a fool understand this.

When the wicked spring as the grass, and when all the workers of iniquity do flourish; it is that they shall be destroyed for ever:

But thou, Lord, art most high for evermore.

For, lo, thine enemies, O Lord, for, lo, thine enemies shall perish; all the workers of iniquity shall be scattered.

But my horn shalt thou exalt like the horn of an unicorn: I SHALL BE ANOINTED WITH FRESH OIL.

Mine eye also shall see my desire on mine enemies, and mine ears shall hear my desire of the wicked that rise up against me.

The righteous shall flourish like the palm tree: he shall grow like a cedar in Lebanon.

*Those that be planted in the house of the Lord
shall flourish in the courts of our God.*
    *They shall still bring forth fruit in old age;
they shall be fat and flourishing;*
    *To shew that the Lord is upright: he is my
rock, and there is no unrighteousness in him.*
— Psalm 92:1-15

This entire Psalm is a psalm of praise to God for His goodness. It begins by saying, *"It is a GOOD thing to give thanks unto the Lord, and to sing praises unto thy name, O most High."*

But notice particularly the latter part of verse 10: *". . . I shall be anointed with fresh oil."* In the midst of praising God for His goodness, the psalmist said, *". . . I shall be anointed with fresh oil."*

In Bible times, particularly in the Old Testament, men were set apart or consecrated to the sacred offices of the prophet, priest, and king by the anointing with oil. Oil is a type of the Holy Spirit. The anointing with oil symbolized that the Holy Spirit would come *upon* men or women to anoint them to stand in a particular office.

Holy Anointing Oil

When the Bible talks about the anointing with oil, it is referring to the actual olive oil along with its various spices and components that was used in Old Testament times to consecrate or set aside someone or something for a holy purpose. As we will see, a person was *anointed* to stand in a particular office or to render special service to God. Also, an object or a thing, for example, such as the

Tabernacle and its furnishings were also *anointed* (Exod. 40:9-15). The anointing oil was *holy oil* and it was used to consecrate or set apart for holy purposes that which the Lord designated.

> EXODUS 30:22-25; 31-33
> 22 Moreover the Lord spake unto Moses, saying,
> 23 Take thou also unto thee principal spices. . . .
> 24 And of cassia . . . and of oil olive. . . .
> 25 And thou shalt make it AN OIL OF HOLY OINT-MENT, an ointment compound after the art of the apothecary: it shall be AN HOLY ANOINTING OIL. . . .
> 31 And thou shalt speak unto the children of Israel, saying, This shall be AN HOLY ANOINTING OIL unto me throughout your generations.
> 32 Upon man's flesh shall it not be poured [that is, it shall be used only upon those whom the Lord designates to be set aside for His purposes, not for common purposes], neither shall ye make any other like it, after the composition of it: IT IS HOLY, and it shall be holy unto you.
> 33 Whosoever compoundeth any like it, or whosoever putteth any of it upon a stranger, shall even be cut off from his people.

The anointing oil was holy because it was a type of the Spirit of God. After the anointing with oil, the Spirit of God would come upon the man of God to anoint him from that day forward to fulfill his office and to carry out God's plan for him on the earth.

Remember that in the Old Testament, people were not born again; therefore, the Holy Spirit could not live *inside* them, He could only come *upon* them to anoint them for service. However, under the New Testament, the Holy Spirit lives *inside* believers (John 14:16,17), and also comes *upon* those who stand in the fivefold ministry gift offices in order to equip them for service (Eph. 4:11,12).

We will see more about the anointing in the life of the believer as we progress in our study.

The Anointing for the Office of the Prophet

In the following scriptures, we see that the anointing oil was used to anoint Elisha to stand in the *prophetic* office. These particular scriptures also mention the anointing with oil for the office of the king, but for our purposes, pay special attention to the anointing with oil for the office of the prophet.

> 1 KINGS 19:15,16; 19-21
> 15 And the Lord said unto him [Elijah the prophet], Go, return on thy way to the wilderness of Damascus: and when thou comest, anoint Hazael to be king over Syria:
> 16 And Jehu the son of Nimshi shalt thou anoint to be king over Israel: and Elisha the son of Shaphat of Abelmeholah shalt thou ANOINT to be PROPHET in thy room. . . .
> 19 So he departed thence, and found Elisha the son of Shaphat, who was plowing with twelve yoke of oxen before him, and he with the twelfth: and Elijah passed by him, and cast his mantle upon him.
> 20 And he left the oxen, and ran after Elijah, and said, Let me, I pray thee, kiss my father and my mother, and then I will follow thee. And he said unto him, Go back again: for what have I done to thee?
> 21 And he returned back from him, and took a yoke of oxen, and slew them, and boiled their flesh with the instruments of the oxen, and gave unto the people, and they did eat. Then he arose, and went after Elijah, and ministered unto him.

Then in Psalm 105:15, the Bible declares that God's

prophets are anointed: ". . . *Touch not mine ANOINTED, and do my PROPHETS no harm.*" God calls His prophets His *anointed.* Old Testament prophets were anointed by the Spirit of God to enable them to stand or function in that particular office.

The Anointing for the Priest's Office

The Bible also talks about the anointing with oil to equip men to stand in the *priest's* office.

EXODUS 29:4-7
4   And Aaron and his sons thou shalt bring unto the door of the tabernacle of the congregation, and shalt wash them with water.
5   And thou shalt take the garments, and put upon Aaron the coat, and the robe of the ephod, and the ephod, and the breastplate, and gird him with the curious girdle of the ephod:
6   And thou shalt put the mitre upon his head, and put the holy crown upon the mitre.
7   Then thou shalt take THE ANOINTING OIL, and pour it upon his head, and ANOINT him.

EXODUS 30:30
30 And thou shalt ANOINT Aaron and his sons, and consecrate them, that they may minister unto me in THE PRIEST'S OFFICE.

The Anointing for the King's Office

Then in First Samuel chapter 16, we see an example of a man of God being anointed to stand or function in the office of king.

1 SAMUEL 16:1-8; 10-13
1   And the Lord said unto Samuel, How long wilt thou mourn for Saul, seeing I have rejected him from reigning

over Israel? fill thine horn with OIL, and go, I will send thee to Jesse the Bethlehemite: for I have provided me a KING among his sons.

2   And Samuel said, How can I go? if Saul hear it, he will kill me. And the Lord said, Take an heifer with thee, and say, I am come to sacrifice to the Lord.

3   And call Jesse to the sacrifice, and I will shew thee what thou shalt do: and thou shalt ANOINT unto me him whom I name unto thee.

4   And Samuel did that which the Lord spake, and came to Bethlehem. And the elders of the town trembled at his coming, and said, Comest thou peaceably?

5   And he said, Peaceably: I am come to sacrifice unto the Lord: sanctify yourselves, and come with me to the sacrifice. And he sanctified Jesse and his sons, and called them to the sacrifice.

6   And it came to pass, when they were come, that he looked on Eliab, and said, Surely the Lord's ANOINTED is before him.

7   But the Lord said unto Samuel, Look not on his countenance, or on the height of his stature; because I have refused him: for the Lord seeth not as man seeth [Isn't that wonderful!]; for man looketh on the outward appearance, but the Lord looketh on the heart.

8   Then Jesse called Abinadab, and made him pass before Samuel. And he said, Neither hath the Lord chosen this. . . .

10 Again, Jesse made seven of his sons to pass before Samuel. And Samuel said unto Jesse, The Lord hath not chosen these.

11 And Samuel said unto Jesse, Are here all thy children? And he said, There remaineth yet the youngest, and, behold, he keepeth the sheep. And Samuel said unto Jesse, Send and fetch him: for we will not sit down till he come hither.

12 And he sent, and brought him in. Now he was ruddy, and withal of a beautiful countenance, and goodly to look to. And the Lord said, Arise, ANOINT him: for this is he.

13 Then Samuel took the horn of OIL, and ANOINTED him in the midst of his brethren: and THE SPIRIT OF THE LORD came upon David from that day forward. . . .

Notice what God said about King David in the Psalms: *"I have found David my servant; with my holy OIL have I ANOINTED him"* (Ps. 89:20). It's the anointing of God which enables a person to stand in the office God has called him to. Also, as we see with David, after he was anointed, the Spirit of the Lord came upon him *from that day forward* to enable him to stand in that office. (1 Sam. 16:13).

Chapter 2
The Anointing in the New Testament

To help us understand the anointing in the New Testament, we must realize that the following are synonymous terms: *power, Spirit, Holy Ghost, Holy Spirit,* and *anointing.* Pay particular attention to this as you read these verses.

The Anointing Upon Jesus

Let's look first at the anointing in Jesus' life. We know that Jesus was born of the Holy Spirit because the Bible clearly indicates this fact. An angel of the Lord appeared to Mary and told her she would give birth to a Son, and that His Name would be called Jesus (Luke 1:31). Thinking in the natural, she said, "... *How shall this be, seeing I know not a man?"* (Luke 1:34). But the angel said that the Holy Spirit or the *power* of God would overshadow Mary.

> **LUKE 1:35**
> **35 ... The HOLY GHOST shall come upon thee, and the POWER of the Highest shall overshadow thee: therefore also that holy thing which shall be born of thee shall be called the Son of God.**

Just as Jesus' birth into this world was a work of the Holy Spirit, the believer's birth into the family of God, the new birth, is accomplished through the work of the Holy Spirit.

Then in Luke chapter 3, we see that thirty years after Jesus' birth, He was anointed with the Holy Spirit. He was endued with power from on High. In other words, He was *anointed* with the Holy Spirit to carry forth His ministry on the earth.

> **LUKE 3:21,22**
> **21 Now when all the people were baptized, it came to pass, that Jesus also being baptized, and praying, the heaven was opened,**
> **22 And the HOLY GHOST descended in a bodily shape like a dove upon him, and a voice came from heaven, which said, Thou art my beloved Son; in thee I am well pleased.**

Thank God for the new birth. But believers also need to be anointed from heaven for service just as Jesus was. When is the believer anointed for service? Jesus said in Acts 1:8, *"But ye shall receive power, after that the Holy Ghost is come upon you: and ye shall be witnesses unto me both in Jerusalem, and in all Judaea, and in Samaria, and unto the uttermost part of the earth."* We see later in Acts 2 when the Holy Spirit descended upon the disciples, that the first thing they did was to go out and bear witness of Jesus. The baptism in the Holy Spirit is the believer's anointing for service.

Here in Luke 3:21,22, we see that Jesus was anointed from on High as the Holy Spirit descended upon him.

Remember also that the words, *power, Spirit, Holy Ghost, Holy Spirit,* and *anointing* are synonymous terms. We see this, for example, in Luke 4:14. After Jesus was anointed by the Holy Spirit at the River Jordan, the Bible says, *". . . Jesus returned in the POWER of the Spirit into Galilee: and there went out a fame of him through all the region round about"* (Luke 4:14).

Immediately after Jesus was anointed by the Holy Spirit, He returned to Galilee in the power of the Spirit because

He was anointed. He returned to His hometown of Nazareth and declared that He was anointed by the Spirit of the Lord. He said, *"The SPIRIT of the Lord is upon me, because he hath ANOINTED me ..."* (Luke 4:18).

Let's look at this passage in its entirety.

LUKE 4:14-21

14 And Jesus returned in the POWER of the Spirit into Galilee: and there went out a fame of him through all the region round about.

15 And he taught in their synagogues, being glorified of all.

16 And he came to Nazareth, where he had been brought up: and, as his custom was, he went into the synagogue on the sabbath day, and stood up for to read.

17 And there was delivered unto him the book of the prophet Esaias. And when he had opened the book, he found the place where it was written,

18 THE SPIRIT OF THE LORD is upon me, because he hath ANOINTED me to preach the gospel to the poor; he hath sent me to heal the brokenhearted, to preach deliverance to the captives, and recovering of sight to the blind, to set at liberty them that are bruised,

19 To preach the acceptable year of the Lord.

20 And he closed the book, and he gave it again to the minister, and sat down. And the eyes of all them that were in the synagogue were fastened on him.

21 And he began to say unto them, This day is this scripture fulfilled in your ears.

Of course we know that the Spirit of the Lord is the Holy Ghost, or the Holy Spirit. So after the Holy Spirit descended upon Jesus and Jesus was anointed from on High, He returned to Galilee in the power of the Holy Spirit; that is, the Holy Spirit came upon Him to anoint Him to fulfill His ministry upon the earth. Notice that it was only after the Holy Spirit descended upon Jesus that Jesus began to declare that He was anointed (v. 18).

Let's look at something else about the anointing in Jesus' life.

We see in the New Testament that Jesus was anointed to stand not only in the prophet's office, but He was also anointed to stand in every one of the fivefold ministry offices listed in Ephesians 4:11, because He had the Spirit without measure.

> EPHESIANS 4:11,12
> 11 And he gave some, APOSTLES; and some, PROPHETS; and some, EVANGELISTS; and some, PASTORS and TEACHERS;
> 12 For the perfecting of the saints, for the work of the ministry, for the edifying of the body of Christ.
>
> JOHN 3:34
> 34 For he whom God hath sent speaketh the words of God: for God giveth NOT THE SPIRIT BY MEASURE UNTO HIM.

Let's look at the various offices Jesus functioned in while He was upon the earth.

Jesus the Apostle

Jesus stood in the office of the apostle. The word "apostle" comes from the Greek word *apostolos* which means *a sent one.* Of course, Jesus stands at the head of the list of "sent ones." In Hebrews 3:1 it says, "*. . . consider the Apostle and High Priest of our profession* [or confession], *Christ Jesus.*"

Jesus the Prophet

We also know Jesus ministered in the office of the

prophet because He called Himself a prophet. He was referring to Himself when He said, *"... A prophet is not
without honour, but in his own country, and among his
own kin, and in his own house"* (Mark 6:4).

Jesus the Evangelist

Jesus ministered in the office of the evangelist, because
He said of Himself, *"The Spirit of the Lord is upon me,
because he hath anointed me to PREACH THE GOS-
PEL ..."* (Luke 4:18). Preaching the gospel message is the
evangelist's primary function, and Jesus specialized in
preaching the gospel.

Jesus the Pastor

Jesus stood in the office of the pastor. The same Greek
word translated "shepherd" is also translated *pastor*. And
Jesus declared about Himself, *"I am the good shepherd:
the good shepherd giveth his life for the sheep"* (John
10:11). Jesus did that, didn't He? He gave His life for the
sheep.

Jesus the Teacher

Jesus also ministered as a teacher because the Word
of God continually makes reference to the fact that Jesus
taught. In fact, if you read through the four Gospels care-
fully and underline the words "teach" or "taught," you'll
find that Jesus' teaching ministry is referred to more than
any other ministry gift He operated in.
   Let's look at several scriptures which show us Jesus'

teaching ministry.

> **LUKE 4:14,15**
> 14 And Jesus returned in the power of the Spirit into Galilee: and there went out a fame of him through all the region round about.
> 15 And he TAUGHT in their synagogues, being glorified of all.
>
> **MATTHEW 7:28,29**
> 28 And it came to pass, when Jesus had ended these sayings, the people were astonished at his DOCTRINE:
> 29 For he TAUGHT them as one having authority, and not as the scribes.

The Anointing Upon Believers

Today we live under the dispensation of the New Covenant; that means we are living under the dispensation of the Holy Spirit. As we have said, the Holy Spirit manifested Himself in the Old Testament, but not to everyone. Not everyone had the anointing of the Spirit of God upon them. Those we would call "laity" didn't have the Spirit of God upon them at all. As we have seen, in the Old Testament only those whom God had particularly selected to stand in certain offices were anointed by the Spirit of God.

The Dual Working of the Holy Spirit
In the Life of the Believer

In the New Testament, however, we need to understand that there is a twofold working of the Holy Spirit in the life of the believer: The Holy Spirit lives *inside* believers, and He also comes *upon* those who stand in the fivefold ministry offices in order to equip them for service.

The Holy Spirit Within

JOHN 14:16,17
16 And I will pray the Father, and he shall give you
another Comforter [the Holy Spirit], that he may abide with
you for ever;
17 Even the Spirit of truth; whom the world cannot receive,
because it seeth him not, neither knoweth him: but ye know
him; for he DWELLETH with you, and shall be IN you.

Then, also, in the New Testament, those believers
whom God calls to the ministry not only have the anointing *in* them as do all believers, but they have the anointing *upon* them as well.

The Holy Spirit Upon

EPHESIANS 4:11,12
11 And he gave some, APOSTLES; and some, PROPHETS;
and some, EVANGELISTS; and some, PASTORS and
TEACHERS;
12 For the perfecting of the saints, FOR THE WORK OF
THE MINISTRY, for the edifying of the body of Christ.

In other words, some are specially anointed to stand
in a particular office such as: apostle, prophet, evangelist,
pastor, or teacher. Or if God calls someone to do a special
work for Him, He'll anoint that person to do that work.
Thank God for the anointing! God will anoint the believer
to fulfill whatever call is on his life.

Now let's go back and trace the anointing in the life
of every believer. Of course, a person first comes into

contact with the anointing when he is born again by the Spirit of God.

> **JOHN 3:5-8**
> 5   Jesus answered, Verily, verily, I say unto thee, Except a man be born of water and OF THE SPIRIT, he cannot enter into the kingdom of God.
> 6   That which is born of the flesh is flesh; and that which is BORN OF THE SPIRIT is spirit.
> 7   Marvel not that I said unto thee, Ye must be born again.
> 8   The wind bloweth where it listeth, and thou hearest the sound thereof, but canst not tell whence it cometh, and whither it goeth: so is every one that is BORN OF THE SPIRIT.

The Great Commission

In the New Testament, born-again believers are anointed by God. What are they anointed to do? First, believers are anointed to tell the good news of the gospel. We see this in the Great Commission.

> **MARK 16:15-18**
> 15 And he said unto them, GO YE INTO ALL THE WORLD, and preach the gospel to every creature.
> 16 He that believeth and is baptized shall be saved; but he that believeth not shall be damned.
> 17 And these signs shall follow them that believe; In my name shall they cast out devils; they shall speak with new tongues;
> 18 They shall take up serpents; and if they drink any deadly thing, it shall not hurt them; they shall lay hands on the sick, and they shall recover.

Jesus said to the disciples, "... *GO YE into all the*

world..." (Mark 16:15). Although Jesus said this to His disciples, the disciples weren't the only ones Jesus was authorizing to preach the gospel; all believers are anointed to carry out the Great Commission. But Jesus was addressing the disciples here because the disciples were the only ministers there were at that time, and they hadn't gone into all the world yet preaching the gospel; they still lived in Jerusalem.

However, later we read in the Acts of the Apostles that when the first great persecution arose, the Early Church was scattered abroad preaching the gospel: "*... at that time there was a great persecution against the church which was at Jerusalem; and they were all scattered abroad throughout the regions of Judaea and Samaria, except the apostles*" (Acts 8:1).

The *"Go ye"* of the Bible is still in effect today! Believers are anointed or commissioned to go into all the world and preach the gospel to every creature.

Authority Given to Believers

Let's look at another scripture which refers to God's anointing believers or giving all believers authority to tell the good news of the gospel.

MARK 13:34,35
34 For the Son of man is as a man taking a far journey, who left his house, and gave AUTHORITY TO HIS SER-VANTS, and to every man his work, and commanded the porter to watch.
35 Watch ye therefore: for ye know not when the master of the house cometh, at even, or at midnight, or at the cock-crowing, or in the morning.

This scripture says, "... *the Son of man is as a man taking a far journey....*" Here Jesus is talking about Himself when He uses the expression "the Son of man." In the New Testament, Jesus is called both the Son of God and the Son of man. From the divine standpoint He is the Son of God. From the human standpoint He is the Son of man.

There is something in this verse for the believer too. Verse 34 says that Jesus gave to every man his "work," and that He commanded the porter to watch. It may be your work just to watch and pray. If it is, be faithful in it and God will reward you.

Notice that the Bible says the Son of man gave "*authority* to His servants." That means as born-again sons of God, we have the authority on the earth to carry out the Great Commission. Jesus said, "*... the Son of man... left his house, and GAVE AUTHORITY TO HIS SERVANTS....*" That's referring to us and to the authority God has given us.

There is another verse which relates to the authority or anointing upon believers to carry out the Great Commission. Remember in Matthew chapter 28, after Jesus rose from the dead, He said that all power or authority was given unto Him. The Greek word translated "power" here also means *authority.* Then in the next verse He immediately authorized the Church to go tell the good news to every nation.

MATTHEW 28:18-20
18 And Jesus came and spake unto them, saying, ALL POWER IS GIVEN UNTO ME in heaven and in earth.
19 GO YE THEREFORE, and teach ALL NATIONS, baptizing them in the name of the Father, and of the Son, and of the Holy Ghost:

20 Teaching them to observe all things whatsoever I have
commanded you: and, lo, I am with you alway, even unto
the end of the world. Amen.

When Jesus said, *"Go ye,"* He was authorizing or com-
missioning the Church, the Body of Christ, to go tell others
about Him. As we've said, Jesus not only said, "Go" to
the disciples, He's saying it to all His disciples everywhere — He's saying it to the whole Church — the entire
Body of Christ. In other words, everywhere we go, we are
to tell the story of Jesus and His redeeming power.

God not only wants us to go tell the good news, but
He wants us to be witnesses endued with *power* from on
High before we go.

LUKE 24:49
49 ... behold, I send the promise of my Father upon you:
but tarry ye in the city of Jerusalem, until ye be endued
with POWER from on high.

ACTS 1:8
8 But ye shall receive POWER, after that the HOLY
GHOST is come upon you: and ye shall be WITNESSES
unto me both in Jerusalem, and in all Judaea, and in
Samaria, and unto the uttermost part of the earth.

Believers are to be endued with power from on High,
just as Jesus was endued with power from on High. However, as we saw, Jesus had the Spirit *without* measure,
and believers receive the Holy Spirit *in a* measure.

JOHN 3:34
34 For he whom God hath sent speaketh the words of God:
for God giveth NOT THE SPIRIT BY MEASURE unto
him.

ROMANS 12:3
3 For I say, through the grace given unto me, to every man that is among you, not to think of himself more highly than he ought to think; but to think soberly, according as God hath dealt to every man THE MEASURE of faith.

So we understand that Jesus told believers to be endued with power from on High so they could be witnesses unto Him, and believers were also authorized or anointed to fulfill the *"Go ye"* of the Great Commission. Every one of us in the Body of Christ is to be a witness!

We know this isn't just referring to the disciples because it wasn't just the 12 disciples who were in the upper room when the anointing came and the Holy Spirit was poured out. The Bible says 120 *believers* were gathered together in that upper room.

ACTS 1:13-15
13 And when they were come in, they went up into an upper room, where abode both Peter, and James, and John, and Andrew, Philip, and Thomas, Bartholomew, and Matthew, James the son of Alphaeus, and Simon Zelotes, and Judas the brother of James.
14 These all continued with one accord in prayer and supplication, with the women, and Mary the mother of Jesus, and with his brethren.
15 And in those days Peter stood up in the midst of the disciples, and said, (the number of names together were about AN HUNDRED AND TWENTY.)

Therefore, all believers are supposed to tell others about Jesus. Does that mean everyone in the Body of Christ is supposed to be a preacher? Emphatically, yes! I didn't say everyone is called to one of the fivefold ministry gifts in the Church (Eph. 4:11). But every Christian is supposed to be a preacher in one sense, because "to preach" means *to proclaim* or *to tell* the good news of Jesus' death, burial, and resurrection. So in that sense, yes, everyone in the Body of Christ is to be a preacher!

As we've seen, Jesus is also anointing people in the Body of Christ today to stand in the fivefold ministry offices of the apostle, prophet, evangelist, pastor, or teacher. However, not everyone in the Body of Christ is called and anointed to stand in one of these offices. But no matter what God calls you to do in life, He will equip you and anoint you to do it.

Chapter 3
New Testament Kings and Priests

God is still anointing prophets and preachers, and He's also still anointing *all* His people to witness about Him. And God is still anointing kings and priests — New Testament kings and priests.

When the word "priests" is mentioned, most people think about the ministry of intercession, because a priest intercedes to God on the behalf of the people.

Under the Old Covenant, the people did not go directly to God for themselves. Every male thirty years of age and older had to present himself in Jerusalem every year. God's Presence was kept shut up in the Holy of Holies in the Temple. Everyone could not go into the Presence of God; only the priests could, and the priests went only with great precaution.

The priest made sacrifice for his sins and for the sins of the people. The blood of innocent animals was shed which was a type of the blood of the sinless, spotless Lamb of God who would one day come and shed His blood for the sins of all people.

The priest entered into that earthly Holy of Holies with the blood of a sacrificial animal, and his sins and the sins of the people were atoned for or "covered" for another year. However, the shedding of the blood of that sacrificial animal did not *cleanse* the sins of the people; it could only *cover* their sins. Then the people could breathe a sigh of relief and go away with their sins atoned for or covered for another year until the next year when again the priest had to present himself in the Holy of Holies for his sins and the sins of the people.

But blessed be God, Jesus our High Priest came and after He died on Calvary and shed His own blood and was raised from the dead, He ascended on High. The Book of Hebrews tells us that He entered into the heavenly Holy of Holies with His own blood to obtain an eternal redemption for us! Now *every* born-again believer can go into the heavenly Holy of Holies and present himself before God anytime he wants to!

A Better Covenant

We can see what a better Covenant we have under the New Testament.

REVELATION 1:1-5
1 The Revelation of Jesus Christ, which God gave unto him, to shew unto his servants things which must shortly come to pass; and he sent and signified it by his angel unto his servant John:
2 Who bare record of the word of God, and of the testimony of Jesus Christ, and of all things that he saw.
3 Blessed is he that readeth, and they that hear the words of this prophecy, and keep those things which are written therein: for the time is at hand.
4 John to the seven churches which are in Asia: Grace be unto you, and peace, from him which is, and which was, and which is to come; and from the seven Spirits which are before his throne;
5 And from Jesus Christ, who is the faithful witness, and the first begotten of the dead, and the prince of the kings of the earth. Unto him that loved us, and WASHED US FROM OUR SINS IN HIS OWN BLOOD.

Under the New Covenant, when we confess our sins, the blood of Jesus actually washes away, remits, or *cleanses* our sins. Thank God, we've been washed from our sins *in His own blood!* (For further study of this subject, *see* Rev. Kenneth E. Hagin's minibook entitled, *Three Big Words.*)

People ask, "Do you understand how that takes place?" No, and you don't either. But I'm rejoicing in it anyway and enjoying the reality of it!

Blood Washed

Jesus washed our sins with His own blood. After our sins were washed in His blood, then as born-again Christians we are made kings and priests unto our God.

> **REVELATION 1:5,6**
> 5 ... Unto him that loved us, and washed us from our sins in his own blood,
> 6 And hath made us KINGS and PRIESTS unto God and his Father; to him be glory and dominion for ever and ever. Amen.

In the Book of Revelation, the Bible tells us that a special millennial reign is coming upon the earth, and that we will reign with Jesus for a thousand years (Rev. 20:7). However, we are already made kings and priests unto God *now* in this life.

> **REVELATION 5:10**
> 10 And hast made us unto our God KINGS and PRIESTS: and we shall reign on the earth.

Romans 5:17 tells us that we already reign and rule in this life as kings and priests.

ROMANS 5:17
17 For if by one man's offence death [that refers to spiritual death] reigned by one; much more they which receive abundance of grace and of the gift of righteousness shall REIGN IN LIFE by one, Jesus Christ.

When shall we reign? In the sweet by and by? No! *In this life!* Another translation reads, "We shall reign as KINGS in life by one, Christ Jesus."

God is still anointing priests and He's still anointing kings. God has anointed you and me — the Body of Christ — to rule and reign as kings and priests unto our God! God also anoints some people to stand in the fivefold ministry, but He has anointed every one of us to preach or to witness about Him.

Every Believer Is Anointed To Be a Priest Unto God

A priest is a go-between — a man or a woman who speaks to God on behalf of others. You don't pray the prayer of intercession for yourself. When you are walking in your rights and privileges in Christ, you know that you can go into the Presence of God. The Word of God says that we are to come boldly to the throne of grace that we may obtain mercy and find grace to help in time of need (Heb. 4:16). An intercessor is one who intercedes on behalf of unbelievers — those who have no rights or privileges to go into the Presence of God for themselves. Some might wonder about praying for other Christians. Isn't that intercession? No, that is supplication. We are exhorted in Scripture to exercise both intercession *and supplication.*

God has anointed every Christian to be a priest.

The Bible doesn't say that only a few in the Body of Christ are made priests unto our God, or that only a few Christians are made kings. No, it says, "... *Unto him that loved us, and washed us from our sins in his own blood,*" and He "... *hath made us kings and priests ...*" (Rev. 1:5,6). Also, the Bible doesn't say that He is *going* to make us kings and priests, but that He has already made us kings and priests unto our God.

God is still anointing His people! He is still anointing kings and priests! God has anointed His people to be priests. A priest speaks to God on behalf of other people. Some people say, "God has called me to be an *intercessor!*" But God has called every one of us to be intercessors. He didn't just call *you.* Intercession is not a *special* calling. Every Christian is supposed to offer intercession and supplication. Some Christians may not have entered into it yet, but they are supposed to. Some have responded more readily to the Holy Spirit than others have, but God has anointed every one of us to be priests unto our God.

The devil thrives on ignorance, and because some people don't know what the Bible says about being priests unto our God, when they do begin to enter into prayer and the anointing comes, then they get lifted up in pride and they think, *I'm somebody! I'm special because I operate in the anointing!*

That's exactly what the devil wants them to think. That's the same way Lucifer sinned. He was lifted up in pride thinking, *I'm special.* He said, "... *I will exalt my throne above the stars of God ... I will be like the most High*" (Isa. 14:13,14). He was lifted up in spiritual pride.

But God has anointed all of His people to be priests unto their God. Instead of thinking they're "special" when they pray, people should just say, "Praise God, we're all anointed to be priests; let's just get after it and pray!"

However, often it seems people — especially those who are not rooted and grounded in the Word of God — tend to get an elevated opinion of themselves and they think they have a special "ministry" or "calling" no one else in the Body of Christ has. They get lifted up in pride and get off into error, thinking they're a special "class" of people, and that no one else in the Body of Christ is like them.

Let's see what the Bible says about the whole Body of Christ being priests unto our God.

> **1 PETER 2:5,9**
> **5   Ye also, as lively stones, are built up a spiritual house, AN HOLY PRIESTHOOD** [That's all of us — the whole Body of Christ!] **to offer up spiritual sacrifices, acceptable to God by Jesus Christ. . . .**
> **9   But ye are a chosen generation, A ROYAL PRIEST-HOOD, an holy nation, a peculiar people; that ye should shew forth the PRAISES of him who hath called you out of darkness into his marvellous light.**

We are all special in the Body of Christ! You see how people can get off into wrong thinking. We are all called to be kings and priests unto our God! Certain ones may be taking advantage of what belongs to them more than others, but our inheritance as kings and priests belongs to all believers.

Another error many Christians have fallen into is that because they think they have a special "calling" or "ministry" to be an intercessor, then they think they've got *to perform* and work something up in the flesh when they pray. Instead of praying in line with the Word of God, and following the leading of the Holy Spirit and praying by the unction and the anointing of the Holy Spirit, they try to perform and work up something in the flesh, and they get off into error. People need to pray in line with the Word of God and by the anointing and unction of the Holy Spirit.

If people do not put the Word of God first — if they do not pray in line with the Word of God — they can go off following what *they* call the "spirit" apart from the Word of God and be misled. You can't follow the Spirit apart from the Word of God because the Spirit and the Word agree (for additional teaching on this subject, *see* Brother Hagin's book, *The Art of Intercession*).

Every Christian is to be a priest! The Bible says, ". . . *ye* [the whole Body of Christ] *are a chosen generation, a royal priesthood, an holy nation, a peculiar people; that ye should shew forth the praises of him who hath called you out of darkness into his marvellous light"* (1 Peter 2:9).

That verse is talking about every one of us in the Body of Christ — not just a few especially "chosen" ones. Every one of us, if we are born again, have been called out of darkness into light, not just a few. You can readily see the error of thinking that only a few *special* members of the Body of Christ are part of this royal priesthood. Some people may not be taking advantage of it, but every one of us is a part of that royal priesthood! God is still anointing priests!

So one function of a priest is to pray for others. What is another function of a priest? As New Testament priests unto our God, we are to continually offer up praises unto the Most High God. (We will look at this in more detail in Chapters 6 and 8.)

The Anointing on Believers To Be Kings

God is not only anointing priests, He's also anointing kings. Who is God anointing to be kings? Every member of the Body of Christ! That means *all* of us!

ROMANS 5:17
17 For if by one man's offence [Adam] death reigned by one [spiritual death]; much more they which receive abundance of grace [the Body of Christ] and of the gift of righteousness SHALL REIGN IN LIFE by one, Jesus Christ.

This verse shows us an area where the Body of Christ is missing it. Most Christians have put off all the reigning until the millennial reign! Thank God, we're going to reign in the Millennium, but on the other hand, the Bible says we are going to reign as kings *now in this life.*

In Revelation 5:10 it says, *"And hast made us unto our God kings and priests: and we shall reign ON THE EARTH."* That not only refers to our reign with Christ in the Millennium, it also refers to our reign on the earth in this life. As we read before, Romans 5:17 says: ". . . We shall reign IN LIFE by Jesus Christ"!

We can see something else about reigning as kings in this life by looking at King David's reign. David as a king living under the Old Testament or Old Covenant didn't try to reign without *the anointing.*

Remember we read that when the priest anointed David to be king, the Bible says the Holy Spirit came on him from that day forward (1 Sam. 16:13). The Spirit of God that came upon David to enable him to reign as king in the Old Testament is the same Holy Spirit that lives inside believers in the New Covenant and enables them to "reign in life by Christ Jesus" (Rom. 5:17). The Spirit of God came upon David for a different purpose — to enable him to rule as the king of Israel, but it's the same Holy Spirit that lives inside believers under the New Covenant.

Many times people get into trouble by trying to reign in the natural. In other words, they try to reign without *the anointing.* But, you see, God is the One who anoints us to reign! Just like He did in the Old Testament, God anoints those of us living under the dispensation of the New Testament too. After all, the Word of God plainly tells us that what happened in the Old Testament is a type and shadow for us in the New Testament, and that we have a better Covenant which is established upon better promises (Heb. 8:6).

How do people try to reign without the anointing? One way is that many people try to live the Christian life without the help and the aid of the Holy Spirit. They try to live the Christian life without the *anointing!* But, first, a person has to be born again in order to live the Christian life. Then as we've seen, Christians need to be endued with power from on High. We will also see that there are *fresh anointings* that all believers are to receive which will enable them to fulfill God's purpose for them on the earth.

Trying 'To Reign' Without Being Born Again!

Over the years, I've had people tell me, "I just can't live the Christian life. I tried it out to see if I could live a holy life, but I can't." Some of the people who said this to me were men whose wives were members of the church I pastored. Their wives had been after them to get saved, so these husbands tried, for example, to quit smoking or drinking for a month or two. Many of these unsaved husbands came back to me and said, "I just can't live the Christian life! There's just no use in me trying to be a Christian."

I've told every single one of them, "You don't have to quit anything in order to become a Christian."

"I don't?"

"No! Just give your life to Jesus!"

"It couldn't be that simple," some have said.

"Yes, it is," I've replied. "When you are born again, God will change you on the *inside!*"

We need to be born again by the Spirit of God! And we need the anointing of the Holy Spirit upon our lives! It's the anointing that will put us over in life.

God is still anointing prophets, preachers, priests, and kings unto our God, and He's still anointing His people to be witnesses for Him!

Chapter 4
Empty Cisterns or Full Reservoirs?

We've looked at the anointing in the Old Testament and in the New Testament. We've seen the anointing with oil in the Old Testament on the prophet, priest, and king. We've looked at the anointing in the New Testament in the life of Jesus and also in the life of the believer. We've seen that God is still anointing all believers with His Holy Spirit to go into all the world to preach the gospel, to witness about Him, and to be New Testament kings and priests unto God.

Now we need to look at another aspect of the anointing.

> **JEREMIAH 2:9-13**
> 9 Wherefore I will yet plead with you, saith the Lord, and with your children's children will I plead.
> 10 For pass over the isles of Chittim, and see; and send unto Kedar, and consider diligently, and see if there be such a thing.
> 11 Hath a nation changed their gods, which are yet no gods? but my people have changed their glory FOR THAT WHICH DOTH NOT PROFIT.
> 12 Be astonished, O ye heavens, at this, and be horribly afraid, be ye very desolate, saith the Lord.
> 13 For my people have committed two evils; they have forsaken me the fountain of living waters, and hewed them out cisterns, BROKEN CISTERNS, that can hold no water.

In this passage of Scripture in Jeremiah, God was speaking to Israel. However, there is also a message in these verses for us, the Church of the Lord Jesus Christ. Here God is saying that Israel committed two evils: One evil was they forsook God, the God of living waters. The second evil was they hewed out for themselves cisterns —

broken cisterns which could hold no water. In other words, they left God's plan and made their own plans. And because their own plans were man-made, they couldn't prosper.

According to the dictionary, a "cistern" is an artificial *reservoir* or *tank,* often located underground for storing rain water. A "reservoir" is a place where water is collected chiefly in large quantities so as to be able to supply the needs of a city or a community, and is kept for use when wanted or needed. In other words, a reservoir is a place where something is collected and stored in large quantities to meet the needs of people.

The Bible is saying in these scriptures that by following man-made plans, Israel hewed out for themselves broken cisterns which couldn't hold water. That is, they exchanged God's glory for that which *couldn't* profit — their own plans and their own way of doing things. They couldn't prosper because they didn't have God's plan. Therefore, we as New Testament believers need to take a lesson from this, and get *God's* plan so we *can* prosper! God doesn't want His people to be empty cisterns; He wants them to be full reservoirs. However, it's up to each one of us in the Body of Christ which one we will be — an empty cistern or a full reservoir.

If we get God's plan, we will be full reservoirs, not empty cisterns which contain nothing but our own plans! Therefore, we need to see what God's New Testament pattern and plan is, so we can get God's plan and prosper. Let's get God's plan! Let's find out what God's plan and provision is for His people to be full reservoirs! I believe God wants every one of His children to be a full reservoir to His glory, don't you?

PSALM 92:10
10 But my horn shalt thou exalt like the horn of an unicorn:
I SHALL BE ANOINTED WITH FRESH OIL.

Believers won't be able to be full reservoirs for God's glory without *the anointing* of God upon their lives. They need to be anointed by the Holy Spirit so that everything they do will prosper as they fulfill God's plan for their individual lives.

How can believers maintain the anointing of God on their lives so they can prosper? The answer to this lies in the fact that believers are to receive a *fresh* anointing to equip them to fulfill God's purposes for them in the earth. The psalmist said, "... *I shall be anointed with fresh oil.*" God wants His people to continually receive *a fresh anointing* so they won't be empty cisterns. And God has made provision for all believers to be full reservoirs at all times, even in the midst of tests and trials. Continually receiving *a fresh anointing* will enable God's people to be *full* reservoirs to His glory.

How can we receive a fresh anointing from God, so we won't be broken, empty cisterns, but we can be full reservoirs unto God's glory? Also, what are the characteristics of those who are full reservoirs — those who maintain a fresh anointing upon their lives? We will be looking at these aspects of the anointing in the following chapters.

If God wants us to be full reservoirs, what does He want us to be full of? First of all, He wants us to be full of the Word of God.

Full of the Word

Christians are to be, first, full of the Word of God. The

Word is *to dwell* or live in us.

> COLOSSIANS 3:16
> 16 Let the word of Christ DWELL in you RICHLY in all
> wisdom. . . .

If the Word is to dwell in us, does the Bible say to what
degree it is to dwell in us? Just a little? To a small degree?
Just enough to get by? No, *richly!* The Word of God is
to dwell in us richly!

Imagine a sponge that is put into water to soak up the
water. We are to "soak up" the Word of God just like a
dry sponge would soak up all the water it can. If you put
a sponge in water, that sponge would get so full of water
that if you touched it anywhere, water would come out.
We are to soak up the Word like that, and get God's Word
into our spirits! Then if we are touched by any circumstances in life, the Word of God will flow out of us just
like water out of a sponge. That's exactly how we are to
be in every situation in life — full of the Word of God!

Soak up the Word until you're so full of the Word that
if you get touched on any side by *any* difficulty, the Word
comes out. If you get touched by persecution, the Word
comes out. If you get touched by criticism, the Word
comes out. If you get touched by tests or trials, the Word
comes out.

There is another area where we are to be so full of the
Word that nothing but the Word comes out.

> ROMANS 12:3
> 3 For I say, through the grace given unto me, to every
> man that is among you, NOT TO THINK OF HIMSELF
> MORE HIGHLY THAN HE OUGHT TO THINK; but to

think soberly, according as God hath dealt to every man the measure of faith.

This verse in Romans says that we are not to think of ourselves more highly than we ought to think. That means we can be so full of God's Word that no matter what touches us in life — even if it is the praise and honor of men — nothing but the Word will flow out of us because that's what's in us! Be so full of the Word that no matter what touches you in life — if it's tests and trials or praise and honor — nothing but the Word of God flows out of you!

COLOSSIANS 3:16
16 Let the word of Christ dwell in you richly IN ALL WISDOM. . . .

Notice something else about this verse in Colossians 3:16. We've determined that the Word of God is to dwell in us richly. But this verse also adds something else: Let the Word of God dwell in you richly *in all wisdom*. The Bible doesn't just say the Word is to dwell in us richly. It says the Word is to dwell in us richly *in all wisdom*.

Why didn't the Bible just say, "Let the Word of Christ *dwell* in you?" Because we need wisdom to know how to rightly divide the Word of God so we can apply it correctly in our lives. The Word of Christ dwells in some people, all right, but they have no wisdom as to how to apply it in its proper context. They misuse the Word and, really, abuse it by taking it out of context and use it to say things it doesn't say. No, the Word of God is to dwell in us richly *in all wisdom*.

Full of the Spirit

What else are Christians to be full of? Full of the Word *first;* then, *second,* full of the Spirit.

To be *full of the Spirit* means to be *fervent* in Spirit.

> **ROMANS 12:10-12**
> **10 Be kindly affectioned one to another with brotherly love; in honour preferring one another;**
> **11 Not slothful in business; FERVENT IN SPIRIT; serving the Lord;**
> **12 Rejoicing in hope; patient in tribulation; continuing instant in prayer.**

You couldn't very well be *fervent* in Spirit without being *filled* with the Holy Spirit, could you?

These scriptures are written to the saints at Rome, but they also apply to the saints of God anywhere. Christians who are living today are just as much beloved of God and called to be saints as the Christians who were living in the days of the Early Church. And in this passage of Scripture the Holy Spirit is admonishing us through Paul to be *fervent* in Spirit as saints of God who possess joint seating in heavenly places with Christ.

This same passage reads a little differently in a number of different translations, which helps bring out the meaning of the verse. As we have seen, *The King James Version* says, "Be fervent in spirit." Other translations read: "Be glowing in spirit" (*The Centenary Translation*); "Have your spirits aglow" (*Weymouth*); "Be on fire with the Spirit" (*Goodspeed*); "Be aglow with the Spirit" (*The Revised Standard Version*); "Be aglow and burning with the Spirit" (*The Amplified Bible*).

To be fervent in Spirit, or to be on fire with the Spirit,

or to be aglow with the Spirit involves both *your* spirit *and* the Holy Spirit; it's not all up to the Holy Spirit. *You* have something to do with being aglow with the Spirit.

But I like one translation better than any of them. It says, "Maintain the spiritual glow" (*Moffatt*). Maintain the glow! God wants us to maintain the glow of the Spirit. You couldn't very well maintain the glow of the Spirit unless you were filled up to overflowing with the Spirit, could you? In other words, God wants us *to stay* filled with the Spirit so we can maintain the spiritual glow of the Spirit.

If God wants us to maintain the glow, then it must be *His will* that we stay *filled* with the Spirit at all times. And the Bible teaches that.

God's Will for Us

EPHESIANS 5:17,18
17 Wherefore be ye not unwise, but UNDERSTANDING WHAT THE WILL OF THE LORD IS.
18 And be not drunk with wine, wherein is excess; but BE FILLED WITH THE SPIRIT.

Is it possible to know what the will of the Lord is? Emphatically, yes! Yet some folks are continually asking, "I wonder what the will of the Lord is for me? I must not be wise because I don't understand what the will of the Lord is for me." But the Holy Spirit through Paul tells us exactly what the will of the Lord is in verse 18.

The will of God for us is *to be filled* with the Spirit! Let's see what being filled with the Spirit involves. For one thing, it means we have to be anointed with *fresh* oil.

PSALM 92:10
10 But my horn shalt thou exalt like the horn of an unicorn:
I SHALL BE ANOINTED WITH FRESH OIL.

I want you to notice that our text said, "I shall be anointed with FRESH oil." That means the psalmist had already been anointed previously with oil. He couldn't very well be anointed with *fresh* oil, unless he's already been anointed with oil some time before, could he?

There is a biblical principle here. After a person is born again, there should be an initial infilling with the Holy Spirit, but then there should be many *refillings* of the Holy Spirit or *fresh* anointings.

It will help us to understand this concept of many refillings of the Holy Spirit, if we understand the Greek translation of Ephesians 5:18, "*Be filled* with the Spirit." Greek scholars tell us that there is actually a play on words in this passage. In the literal Greek, "Be filled with the Spirit," actually translates, "Be *being* filled with the Spirit."

In other words, Paul is saying, "Maintain a constant experience of being filled with the Holy Spirit." Paul is encouraging Christians to stay filled with the Spirit — to continue to have a fresh anointing of the Holy Spirit in their lives. We will now look at New Testament examples of the Early Church receiving *a fresh anointing.*

Chapter 5
New Testament Pattern

Let's look at several New Testament examples of *be being* filled with the Holy Spirit or being continually anointed with *fresh* oil. We can see this pattern in the New Testament of an initial infilling of the Holy Spirit and numerous refillings, for example, in Acts 2:1-4 and Acts 4:23-31.

> ACTS 2:1-4
> 1 And when the day of Pentecost was fully come, they were all with one accord in one place.
> 2 And suddenly there came a sound from heaven as of a rushing mighty wind, and it filled all the house where they were sitting.
> 3 And there appeared unto them cloven tongues like as of fire, and it sat upon each of them.
> 4 And THEY WERE ALL FILLED WITH THE HOLY GHOST, and began to speak with other tongues, as the Spirit gave them utterance.

In this passage we see that the 120 persons who were gathered together in Jerusalem were *filled* with the Holy Spirit. They were anointed with the oil of the Holy Spirit from on High in the baptism of the Holy Spirit and they spoke with other tongues.

Then in Acts 2:46,47, we read that the Lord added to the church daily such as should be saved. When this occurred, a number of days had passed since the day of Pentecost.

> ACTS 2:46,47
> 46 And they, continuing daily with one accord in the

temple, and breaking bread from house to house, did eat
their meat with gladness and singleness of heart,
47 Praising God, and having favour with all the people.
And the Lord added to the church daily such as should be
saved.

Then we come to Acts chapter 3 where Peter and John
were going into the Temple. There was a lame man at the
Gate Beautiful who was healed. You remember the story.
Peter spoke to the lame man and said, *"Silver and gold
have I none; but such as I have give I thee: In the name
of Jesus Christ of Nazareth rise up and walk"* (Acts 3:6).
The lame man was healed, and went into the Temple with
them, *". . . walking, and leaping, and praising God."* (v. 8).

After the lame man was healed, Peter and John were
taken into custody and questioned by the priests and the
rulers of the Temple. The Jewish leaders threatened the
disciples not to speak or teach in the Name of Jesus. Then
they let them go (*See* Acts chapters 3 and 4).

ACTS 4:23-31
23 And being let go, they [the disciples] went to their own
company, and reported all that the chief priests and elders
had said unto them.
24 And when they heard that, they lifted up their voice
to God with one accord, and said, Lord, thou art God, which
hast made heaven, and earth, and the sea, and all that in
them is:
25 Who by the mouth of thy servant David hast said, Why
did the heathen rage, and the people imagine vain things?
26 The kings of the earth stood up, and the rulers were
gathered together against the Lord, and against his Christ.
27 For of a truth against thy holy child Jesus, whom thou
hast anointed, both Herod, and Pontius Pilate, with the
Gentiles, and the people of Israel, were gathered together,

28 For to do whatsoever thy hand and thy counsel determined before to be done.
29 And now, Lord, behold their threatenings: and grant unto thy servants, that with all boldness they may speak thy word,
30 By stretching forth thine hand to heal; and that signs and wonders may be done by the name of thy holy child Jesus.
31 And WHEN THEY HAD PRAYED, the place WAS SHAKEN where they were assembled together; and they were all FILLED WITH THE HOLY GHOST, and they spake the word of God with boldness.

In verse 31, we see that those who were gathered to pray were filled with the Holy Ghost. But we read that these Christians were already filled with the Holy Ghost in Acts 2:4. Yes, these Christians were initially filled with the Holy Spirit in Acts chapter 2, but in Acts 4:31 they received a *refilling* of the Holy Spirit — a fresh anointing. Remember, the psalmist said, "I will be anointed with *fresh* oil."

These early Christians were anointed with fresh oil, all right! Look at verse 31: "*. . . the place WAS SHAKEN where they were assembled together. . . .*" The anointing was so strong, the place where they were gathered was shaken. That means the whole house shook!

There was such a manifestation of God's power that the very building where they were gathered together to pray was shaken, and they were all filled up to overflowing with the Holy Spirit. They got a fresh anointing!

There is one initial filling with the Holy Ghost, but many refillings. And that's where some folks have missed it. Just because you got filled with the Spirit perhaps years ago, it's not a past experience that's going to put you over in life.

D. L. Moody once said, "People living on past experiences are living on stale manna."

Years ago I heard a man say, "I was saved in 1919, baptized with the Holy Ghost in 1919, and spoke with other tongues!" But that was as far as he ever went with God; he'd been as "dead as a mackerel" ever since! We need to ask ourselves, *What about now? What's my testimony now? Am I filled with the Holy Spirit now?*

Let's look at another New Testament example of Christians receiving a fresh anointing.

In Acts 19 we see that the Christians in Ephesus were initially filled with the Holy Spirit under Paul's ministry.

ACTS 19:1-6
1 ... Paul having passed through the upper coasts came to Ephesus: and finding certain disciples,
2 He said unto them, Have ye received the Holy Ghost since ye believed? And they said unto him, We have not so much as heard whether there be any Holy Ghost.
3 And he said unto them, Unto what then were ye baptized? And they said, Unto John's baptism.
4 Then said Paul, John verily baptized with the baptism of repentance, saying unto the people, that they should believe on him which should come after him, that is, on Christ Jesus.
5 When they heard this, they were baptized in the name of the Lord Jesus.
6 And when Paul had laid his hands upon them, the HOLY GHOST came on them; and THEY SPAKE WITH TONGUES, and prophesied.

When Paul initially came to Ephesus, these folks hadn't heard that Jesus had come; they had not been born again and, therefore, had not received the baptism in the Holy Spirit. All they knew about was John's baptism in water.

Paul told them about Jesus — about His death on the Cross, His burial, His resurrection, and His ascension on High.

Paul explained to these Ephesians that what they had as a promissory note through John the Baptist, they could now receive as a reality in their lives through Jesus Christ. John the Baptist had preached, *"I indeed have baptized you with water: but he* [Jesus] *shall baptize you with the Holy Ghost"* (Mark 1:8). They received Jesus and were filled with the Holy Spirit (Acts 19:5,6).

Then in Ephesians chapter 5, Paul writes this same group of people and tells them to be *filled* with the Spirit.

> EPHESIANS 1:1
> 1   Paul, an apostle of Jesus Christ by the will of God, TO THE SAINTS which are AT EPHESUS, and to the faithful in Christ Jesus.
>
> EPHESIANS 5:18
> 18 And be not drunk with wine, wherein is excess; but BE FILLED WITH THE SPIRIT.

Paul said to the Ephesian Christians, *". . . be not drunk with wine . . . be filled with the Spirit"* (v. 18). In saying this, Paul is not telling these Christians to receive the baptism of the Holy Spirit again; they had already received the Holy Spirit as recorded in Acts 19:1-6.

No, Paul is writing to these same born-again, Spirit-filled saints in Ephesus and he's instructing and encouraging them to be *being* filled with the Spirit. In other words, he's telling them to maintain a constant experience of being filled with the Holy Spirit. He's giving them further instruction on the Spirit-filled life and how to walk in the fullness of God's will by staying filled up to overflowing with the Holy Spirit.

You see, Paul is talking about a continual experience of being filled with the Holy Spirit. He's saying, *"Stay filled with the Spirit. Get anointed anew with fresh oil! Don't be drunk with wine, but be filled to overflowing with the Spirit"* (Eph. 5:18).

There is one initial filling in the baptism of the Holy Spirit, but there are to be many refillings of the Holy Spirit. It comes back to this: Are Christians following God's New Testament pattern by staying filled with the Holy Spirit? Are God's people *maintaining* the spiritual glow of the Spirit in their lives by *staying* full of the Holy Spirit? Are they fervent in Spirit? *Are they empty cisterns or are they full reservoirs?*

For example, we know that if a person gets full of wine, he gets drunk. Water is a type of the Holy Spirit, just as wine is used in the Bible as a type of the Holy Spirit. The Bible says, *". . . be not drunk with wine . . . but be FILLED with* [or drunk on] *the Spirit"* (Eph. 5:18). The Bible is using the example of someone who is so *full* of wine that he's drunk. For someone to stay drunk on wine, he would have to keep on drinking, wouldn't he? And just because he initially got drunk, doesn't mean he's going to be drunk next week — unless he drinks again.

Christians are not to be drunk with wine, but they *are* to be filled with the Spirit. If you get full of the Holy Ghost, you get drunk too — on the Spirit. But just because you were initially filled with the Holy Spirit and spoke with other tongues, doesn't mean you're filled up to overflowing *today* on the Spirit. Vessels can leak. That's why we need to stay *continually filled* with the Holy Spirit *every*

day. We're to get full of or *drunk on* the Holy Spirit today.
We need a fresh anointing today. Then we're to get drunk
on the Holy Spirit this week, and next week, and the week
after that. We're to stay *full* of the Holy Spirit!

Get drunk *on the Spirit!* Stay in God's Presence long
enough to get a fresh anointing — until you get filled to
overflowing in the Spirit. God's people need a fresh
anointing!

The Church Today

I think that is where we are missing it in the Church
today. Christians aren't staying filled up to overflowing
with the Holy Spirit. They don't understand that they are
to stay in God's Presence and stay in the Word of God
until they get a fresh anointing. There is one initial infilling of the Holy Spirit in the baptism of the Holy Spirit,
but Christians cannot be full reservoirs without numerous
refillings. If these Christians here in Ephesians needed to
be filled again, we need to be too.

You hear so-called "faith" people say, "I've been filled
with the Holy Spirit. I'm making all the right confessions,
and I'm believing God, but nothing is happening!" Yes,
they may have received the initial infilling of the Holy
Spirit, all right. But over the process of time, water leaks
out of a vessel, and when that happens, in the process of
time — amidst the tests and trials of life — if you don't
stay filled up with the Spirit, it's possible to become an
empty cistern instead of a full reservoir. You have to keep
refilling a vessel to keep it full of water, so it can be a *full*
reservoir because water evaporates and can leak out.

Stay drunk on the Spirit of God! You can get so drunk

on the Holy Ghost that you stagger around like a drunk man. Get filled up and stay filled to overflowing with the Holy Spirit! There's one initial filling, but there are to be many refillings — many fresh anointings.

I don't know too much about people being drunk. I haven't been around many people who were drunk. On one occasion, I remember I was visiting some folks, and the man's boss came to dinner. This fellow was a new convert and perhaps not yet as developed as he should have been in his understanding in certain areas. When he arrived for dinner, he had been drinking and was a little intoxicated. He laughed all through the meal. He would ask for corn instead of potatoes, or rice instead of beans, and then he'd just laugh.

I thought about this scripture in Ephesians 5:18, "Be not drunk with wine, but be drunk on the Spirit." When you get drunk *on the Spirit,* you laugh and don't have a care in the world. You talk about getting high in the Spirit! When you're full of God's Spirit, natural things just look different. You're full of thanksgiving and your heart continuously has a song unto the Lord.

Have you ever noticed that when you're drunk on the Holy Spirit, natural things look different? You'll find that many people you may have thought were *un*attractive, look attractive when you get filled with the Holy Ghost. Things just look better when you're filled to overflowing with the Holy Spirit! You see people through the eyes of the love of God, so to speak. Some of the most marvelous things happen when you're *filled up* with the Spirit.

The Anointing Changes Things

We were holding a meeting in a certain city and as some

of the singers got to singing, the anointing of God came into that building in a glorious way. The joy of the Lord so filled that place that I began to laugh. Then the singers began to laugh too, and we all just began to laugh in the Spirit.

There was a woman in the service who later told us that one of her sons wasn't just exactly where he should be with God; he happened to be sitting outside that meeting in a parked truck.

After the meeting, he told his mother that something had happened to him while the service was in progress. He'd had an experience with God. He said to his mother, "Momma, I could hear those singers laughing, and when they got to laughing, it was like a thick cloud came into the truck and filled and enveloped it."

The Presence of God came into that truck like a cloud, and this young man got right with God! He had been born again some time before, and although he'd had some fellowship with God, he wasn't walking with the Lord as he should have been.

His mother told us later, "He has never been the same since that experience! His relationship is totally restored with the Lord, and he's been walking with the Lord ever since. He dedicated and consecrated his life to God!" All we were doing was just laughing in the Spirit — because we were so *filled* with the Spirit — filled to overflowing with the joy of the Lord.

I've seen some of the greatest things happen when people were filled up — like a *full* reservoir — with the Spirit of God. Not an empty cistern, but a full reservoir! Full of the Holy Spirit! Pastors should get so full of the Holy Spirit that their churches are full reservoirs to spiritually feed and water a whole city!

Now let's look again at our New Testament pattern.

> ACTS 4:31
> 31 And when they had prayed, the place was shaken where they were assembled together; and they were all filled with the Holy Ghost, and they spake the word of God with boldness.

When the Early Church received a fresh anointing of the Holy Spirit here in Acts 4:31, the whole building where they were praying was shaken. They got so full, the building shook! That happened because the Holy Spirit not only filled them, but He also filled the room where they were praying.

I was raised Southern Baptist and in the course of time I got filled with the Holy Ghost and spoke with other tongues. I knew nothing about the move of the Spirit. Eventually, I came over among the Pentecostals, and in meetings I'd see folks raise their hands and sometimes their hands would just shake under the power of the Holy Spirit.

Since then I've been in services where the power of God was in manifestation so powerfully that the very atmosphere seemed charged with the power of God. When I'd lift my hands to praise God, it just seemed as if there was "electricity" in the air — the very atmosphere was charged with the anointing of God. When the Holy Spirit starts moving, the anointing will affect you physically as well as spiritually.

Some folks get excited sometimes about people falling under the power, or shaking under the power. But wait until the building starts shaking! Then they will really get excited!

If Christians in the Early Church needed a refilling, then we need a refilling too. That is one of our problems in the Church today. We need a fresh anointing!

How long has it been since you've been filled up to overflowing with the Holy Spirit? How long has it been since you received a fresh anointing of the Holy Spirit?

One Accord

How do Christians get a fresh anointing? How did these Christians get a fresh anointing in the Early Church? For example, how did that fresh anointing come upon those disciples in Acts chapter 4?

> ACTS 4:23,24,31
> 23 And being let go, they went to their own company [That's where some Christians are missing it; they don't have a company — a local body — to go to when they get in trouble.], and reported all that the chief priests and elders had said unto them.
> 24 And when they heard that, they lifted up their voice to God WITH ONE ACCORD, and said, Lord, thou art God, which hast made heaven, and earth, and the sea, and all that in them is. . . .
> 31 And when they had prayed, THE PLACE WAS SHAKEN where they were assembled together; and they were ALL FILLED WITH THE HOLY GHOST, and they spake the word of God with boldness.

For one thing, notice that they were all gathered together in prayer *in one accord.* I sometimes think we've lost a lot in some of our big meetings where we don't have room for folks to gather around the altar and pray. Of course, not every service needs to be conducted in this fashion. On the other hand, I think we're missing out on some of the "*be being* filled" with the Spirit by not taking time or having the facilities to pray together in one accord as a church family in some of our church services. It used to be that you'd give an altar call and people would come around the altar and kneel down and pray. With people praying together like that in one accord, everyone got anointed with fresh oil!

Here in Acts 4:31, when the people were all praying in one accord, *all* the people — every single Christian in that place — was filled up to overflowing in the Holy Spirit *with a fresh anointing.* Yes, we can all pray separately at home, and we ought to do that. But there's just something about united prayer that brings the power of God in demonstration in a greater measure.

Chapter 6
Characteristics of Those
With a Fresh Anointing

How many of our problems would be solved in the church today if Christians had a fresh anointing of the Holy Spirit upon their lives! You see, by not maintaining a constant experience of being filled to overflowing with the Spirit, many times Christians go through problems and face trials in life they wouldn't have to face if they were *filled up* with the Spirit.

That doesn't mean there won't be tests and trials in life. No, the Bible doesn't teach that. Tests and trials come to us all in life. But when you stay filled with the Holy Spirit and the Word of God, there will be some tests and trials in life that you will never have to experience. Stay in the Presence of God until you get a fresh anointing!

We have seen from the Scriptures that it is God's will for His people to be filled with the Spirit. That is, Christians are to maintain a constant experience of being filled with the Spirit so they can be full reservoirs instead of empty cisterns.

Now let's look at the *characteristics* of those who are continually *"be being* filled" with the Spirit. We need to see the results of being anointed with fresh oil and the characteristics of those who *maintain* a fresh anointing of the Holy Spirit in their lives.

EPHESIANS 5:18-21
18 And be not drunk with wine, wherein is excess; but be [being] FILLED with the Spirit;
19 SPEAKING to yourselves in psalms and hymns and

spiritual songs, SINGING and MAKING MELODY in
your heart to the Lord;
20 GIVING THANKS ALWAYS FOR all things unto
God and the Father in the name of our Lord Jesus Christ;
21 SUBMITTING YOURSELVES one to another in the
fear of God.

Supernatural Utterance

First, notice verse 19: *"Speaking to yourselves. . . ."*
Have you ever noticed in connection with being filled with
the Spirit how many times the Bible talks about *speaking? ". . . be filled with the Spirit; SPEAKING . . ."*
(vv. 18,19). In other words, the result of being filled with
the Spirit is speaking in a supernatural utterance. Let's
look at those verses which show us this.

ACTS 2:4
4   And they were all FILLED with the Holy Ghost, and
began to SPEAK with other tongues, as the Spirit gave
them utterance.

ACTS 10:44-46
44 While Peter yet spake these words, the Holy Ghost fell
on all them which heard the word.
45 And they of the circumcision which believed were
astonished . . . because that on the Gentiles also was poured
out the gift of the Holy Ghost.
46 For they heard them SPEAK with tongues, and
magnify God. . . .

ACTS 4:31
31 And when they had prayed, the place was shaken where
they were assembled together; and they were all FILLED
with the Holy Ghost, and they SPAKE the word of God
with boldness.

EPHESIANS 5:18,19
18 ... be [being] FILLED with the Spirit;
19 SPEAKING to yourselves in psalms and hymns and
spiritual songs. ...

Speaking supernaturally is speaking by the unction of
the Holy Spirit. When you get filled with the Holy Spirit,
you speak with tongues. And in order to maintain the
Spirit-filled life you ought to keep on speaking in tongues.
You can also speak supernaturally in psalms, hymns, and
spiritual songs by the unction of the Spirit. We will see
this as we study Ephesians 5:18 and 19. And we see here
that the disciples spoke the Word of God with boldness;
we will see that speaking the Word of God with boldness
is a result of being *filled* with the Spirit. All of these are
examples of supernatural *speaking;* that is, speaking by
the unction and the anointing of the Holy Spirit.

Now let's look at Ephesians 5:18-21 again to see the
other characteristics of one who is filled with the Spirit.
Notice particularly the words: *Speaking, singing, giving
thanks,* and *submitting.*

EPHESIANS 5:18-21
18 ... be [being] FILLED with the Spirit;
19 SPEAKING to yourselves in psalms and hymns and
spiritual songs, SINGING and making melody in your
heart to the Lord;
20 GIVING THANKS always for all things unto God and
the Father in the name of our Lord Jesus Christ;
21 SUBMITTING yourselves one to another in the fear
of God.

We've seen that a characteristic of one who stays filled
with the Holy Spirit is speaking in tongues. We can also

see by Ephesians 5:19 that to maintain a fresh anointing upon your life, you can speak to yourself in psalms, hymns, and spiritual songs which also come by supernatural utterance. If you are filled up to overflowing with the Spirit — if you maintain a fresh anointing of God upon your life — you will also continually be *giving thanks* unto God, and you will have a humble and *submissive spirit or attitude* toward others.

Singing

When the Bible talks about psalms, hymns, and spiritual songs, it's not referring to singing songs out of a songbook. It is talking about a supernatural utterance given by the spirit of prophecy. Psalms, hymns, and spiritual songs are given by the inspiration of the Holy Spirit at the spur of the moment; they are not learned or rehearsed.

We remember that prophecy is inspired utterance in a known tongue, and that the simple gift of prophecy is given "to speak to men unto edification, and exhortation, and comfort" (1 Cor. 14:3). The Bible says, *"For ye may all prophesy . . ."* (1 Cor. 14:31). The simple gift of prophecy is not to be confused with *the ministry of a prophet*. We know that every Christian can be filled with the Spirit and prophesy, but not all Christians are called to stand in the office of the prophet. But because *every* member of the Body of Christ can prophesy, *any* member of the Body of Christ can speak or sing in psalms, hymns, and spiritual songs because they are given by the Holy Spirit through the spirit of prophecy.

Remember also the Bible says, ". . . *out of the*

abundance of the heart the mouth speaketh" (Matt. 12:34).
Whatever is in your heart is going to come out of your
mouth. If you've got a song in your heart, it's going to
come out. If it's not coming out of your mouth, it's just
not in your heart. But if you're filled with the Spirit, you've
got a song in your heart, and it will eventually come out
of your mouth!

Now let's look again at Ephesians 5:18,19, and its companion verse, Colossians 3:16 to understand more about
speaking or singing in psalms, hymns, and spiritual songs.

> **EPHESIANS 5:18,19**
> 18 ... be [being] filled with the Spirit;
> 19 **SPEAKING TO YOURSELVES** in psalms and hymns
> and spiritual songs, singing and making melody in your
> heart **TO THE LORD.**

There are two things I want you to notice in this verse.
First, in verses 18 and 19 the Bible is talking about speaking in psalms and hymns in your own private life at home.
It says, *"Speaking to yourselves ... [and] to the Lord."*
As we said, these are songs that the Holy Ghost gives you
by the inspiration of the Spirit, not necessarily those you
get out of a songbook. A psalm is a spiritual poem or an
ode. You speak or sing these psalms and spiritual songs
to yourself, to edify and build yourself up.

The companion scripture to this verse, Colossians 3:16,
gives us some further instruction on speaking in psalms
and hymns and spiritual songs.

> **COLOSSIANS 3:16**
> 16 Let the word of Christ dwell in you richly in all wisdom;
> teaching and admonishing **ONE ANOTHER** in psalms and
> hymns and spiritual songs, singing with grace in your
> hearts to the Lord.

We've already looked at this verse in relation to being filled with the Word of God: *"Let the word of Christ dwell in you richly in all wisdom...."* But there's something else I want you to notice about this verse.

Here in Colossians 3:16, the Bible is talking about teaching and admonishing *one another.* Notice that we are also to *teach* and *admonish* one another in psalms, hymns, and spiritual songs. We are to minister to one another, *teaching* and *admonishing* one another in psalms and hymns and spiritual songs.

That means if you didn't know what the psalm or hymn is instructing — then it's *teaching* you; you're being *taught* what is given by the inspiration of the Holy Spirit. If you did know it, then the psalm, hymn, or spiritual song is *admonishing* you. However, we won't be able to teach and admonish one another in psalms, hymns, and spiritual songs unless the word of Christ dwells in us richly in all wisdom!

According to Colossians 3:16 then, there are some psalms, hymns, and spiritual songs that are to be spoken or sung *to one another.* And yet, on the other hand, the Bible says in Ephesians 5:19 there are some psalms, hymns, and spiritual songs that we are to speak *to ourselves,* singing with grace in our hearts *to the Lord.* Therefore, there are some songs, hymns, and spiritual songs we are to sing to one another, and there are some we are to sing to ourselves and unto the Lord.

Colossians 3:17 sheds more light on this for us.

COLOSSIANS 3:17
17 And whatsoever ye do in word or deed, do all in the name of the Lord Jesus, giving thanks to God and the Father by him.

Whether we speak or sing in psalms, hymns, and spiritual songs in our own private devotions to build ourselves up and to sing unto the Lord, or whether we speak or sing them to teach and admonish one another in the public assembly — let everything be done as unto the Lord to glorify His Name.

Sometimes I just *speak* in psalms because I'm not a singer; otherwise, I would sing the psalms the Holy Spirit gives me. But since I don't sing, I just recite the psalm or the hymn that comes by the inspiration of the Spirit. The Bible says to speak *to yourself* in psalms, hymns, and spiritual songs and to have a song in your heart to the Lord. I sometimes wake up at 4 o'clock in the morning, and just spend an hour or two speaking to myself in psalms. We're all encouraged to do that.

Don't Stop at the Door to the Supernatural!

So many times folks have just stopped at the door to the supernatural. They got filled with the Holy Ghost and they spoke with other tongues. Thank God for that. But there is more to the supernatural power of God than that. If you were initially filled with the Holy Spirit and spoke in tongues, then continue to speak supernaturally — both in tongues and in psalms, hymns, and spiritual songs. And stay filled with the Word of God so you can speak it forth boldly.

Staying full of the Word and full of the Spirit is how we constantly maintain a fresh anointing in our lives. We need to stay in God's Presence until we get a fresh anointing. We need to follow God's New Testament pattern so we can be full reservoirs to His glory.

So let's continue to speak with other tongues and to sing and make melody in our hearts to the Lord. And let's continue to teach and admonish one another because the Word of Christ dwells in us richly in all wisdom.

When was the last time you spoke in a psalm given by the inspiration of the Holy Spirit? Maybe you've said, "I've heard other Christians speak in psalms, and I've prayed that the Lord would give that ability to me." Or maybe you've thought that speaking in psalms, hymns, and spiritual songs belongs to just a *few* Christians and that not every Christian has the ability to speak in psalms. But, no, as we've seen speaking by the unction of the Spirit belongs to every single Christian because the Bible said, "Ye may all prophesy." And speaking in psalms, hymns, and spiritual songs is exercising the simple gift of prophecy.

God is still anointing His people to prophesy! I'm not talking about standing in the office of the prophet. I'm talking about the simple gift of prophecy. The Bible says the simple gift of prophecy is to speak to men unto edification, exhortation, and comfort, and that we may all prophesy: "... *ye may all prophesy one by one* ..." (1 Cor. 14:31).

But, you see, even the simple gift of prophecy must be exercised under the anointing. So much of the time people don't prophesy under *the anointing;* they work up something in the flesh. No, they need to wait for the anointing to prophesy. They need to be anointed with fresh oil!

Therefore, if you're full of the Holy Spirit — if you're anointed with fresh oil — you can speak to yourself and to the Lord in psalms, hymns, and spiritual songs whenever you desire. If it weren't possible to do so, the Bible wouldn't encourage us to do it! We all need to be anointed with the fresh oil that speaking with psalms, hymns, and spiritual songs brings.

We're to speak to whom? To yourself *and* to the Lord! Whether you are by yourself or with someone else, stay in God's Presence long enough to be filled with a fresh anointing, speaking in psalms and hymns and spiritual songs in your heart to the Lord. Then you will be filled to overflowing with the Spirit of God and you can teach and admonish one another.

The anointing to speak in psalms, hymns, and spiritual songs will come up inside of you. The Holy Spirit is in you, and the anointing of God is in you too. Sometimes the anointing will come upon you; sometimes it will rise up within you. It works in different ways with different people, but it is still the same anointing. When that anointing comes upon you or rises up within you, the words will just come rolling out of your mouth and you will speak words unto God you never thought of speaking before. There will be a certain amount of rhyme to them because a psalm is a spiritual poem or ode. It may rhyme or it may not, but there is an element of poetry to it.

When I get started speaking in that realm, psalms just keep flowing out of me. I have spoken nearly all night long just to myself in psalms. Here are two of the psalms the Holy Spirit has given me.

Praising the Lord

I will praise the Lord at all times;
I am not moved by what I see.
When the way seems dark,
when there seems no way,
I stand my ground and praise Him;
Because He seeth the way that I go and I walk in His path,

and I'll do that which is pleasing in His sight.

And the storms of life may come,
and the thunder may roll and the lightning may flash,
but as I walk, I know that victory is mine at last!

Because, you see, He came from heaven long ago,
and He is the Champion sent by the Father God
to the earth below, and He elevates mankind
into the place where they know —
Know their place in Him!
Know the reality of His blessings and truth.
And so the enemy cannot gainsay them.
And they'll praise God day and night.

Victory

Victory is not in places or things.
Victory is not in what I can see or feel.
Victory is in Him — Christ the Champion from heaven.

He came from the bosom of the Father to the earth,
and took my place and became my Substitute.
And defeated the enemy in his own domain.

Jesus arose victorious with the keys of heaven
and the keys of hell and death,
and invited all to come and go with Him to heaven.

Bubbling Up on the Inside

Stay filled with the Spirit! Stay in God's Presence and

stay full of the Word until you get a fresh anointing. Stay in God's Presence until the anointing just comes bubbling up from inside of you.

Have you ever heard a whistling tea kettle? When you put water on the stove to heat in a tea kettle, that water is not hot enough just because the tea kettle lets off one or two little whistles. To get that water really hot, you let the teapot stay on the fire until that water just begins bubbling up and there's a steady flow of steam coming out!

If you'll stay in God's Presence long enough to get anointed with fresh oil, the anointing will come bubbling up on the inside. Then a steady stream of prayer, praise, and thanksgiving to God will flow out of your lips! Speaking in psalms comes up out of your spirit. It may be that you'll speak in psalms by the simple gift of prophecy in your own language. Or maybe you will speak in tongues and the interpretation will be in psalms. But it will all come flowing out of your spirit as you stay in God's Presence and get a fresh anointing!

Notice another aspect of Ephesians 5:19: "... *singing and making melody in your heart to the Lord.*" When you speak in psalms and hymns and you are singing and making melody in your heart to the Lord, you're ministering to the Lord.

God wants us to maintain a spirit of praise to Him continually because as we saw in Chapter 3, the Bible says we are priests unto God; priests are to offer the sacrifice of praise to God continually. We are to continually have a song in our hearts so we can offer praise unto God. That is ministering unto the Lord.

Because you're filled with the Spirit, you're singing — you've got a song in your heart. In other words, you've got a song on the inside. And if you stay filled with the Spirit, you will have a fresh anointing in your life, and nothing can stop you from singing!

It may seem that you just got the worst news that you could ever get, but if you're filled with the Spirit, you've got a song in your heart no matter what the circumstances of life may be. If you have a song in your heart, nothing can stop you from singing. You'll laugh right in the face of the devil. You'll laugh and sing and be happy, not *because of* the trials you might be going through, but *in spite of* any trials or circumstances, which would defeat ordinary people.

But we're not ordinary people. We're *Spirit-filled* people. We're supernatural people. That word "supernatural" means we're *beyond the natural*. The natural shouldn't affect us as it does folks living in the natural. The natural course of events doesn't have to pull us down; circumstances can't get us down if we're filled up with the Spirit and we have a song in our hearts. Because we are supernatural people, we are to get a fresh anointing and maintain the glow right in the midst of adverse circumstances.

Chapter 7
Maintaining the Glow
In Adverse Circumstances

Some folks who have taught the so-called "faith message" maybe haven't put the emphasis where it should be put. Some people seem to think if you believe God, nothing bad is ever going to happen to you. Some people have taught that if you have faith, you're just going to float through life on flowery beds of ease.

But if you live for God, sometimes you've got to swim upstream, not just float downstream! In life there will be those times you will have to swim upstream! Sometimes it seems that everything else is going the opposite way and you have to swim upstream! Walking by faith is not always easy.

I remember some experiences I've had along this line after God called me into the field ministry in 1949 and 1950. In those first few years, God told me for a while just to stay and preach in the churches. I'm out to obey God, so I stayed in the churches and held what we call Church meetings or revival meetings.

I remember one particular pastor asked me to come and hold a meeting for him. I thought, *Dear Lord, I don't want to hold a meeting for that pastor.* At a convention right in front of everyone, I had heard him criticize people who taught about faith and healing, and for ministering in the Spirit like I did in healing services by the gifts of the Spirit.

At the time I thought, *Doesn't he know I minister like that?* Some time after he said that, he invited me to come and hold a meeting in his church. I prayed, "Lord, I don't want to go minister at his church because I know that what I teach about faith and healing would be plowing his field crossways. He's been making furrows up and down one way, and if I come to his church I'm going to make furrows up and down the other way. Surely you don't want me to go to his church!"

The Lord said, "I want you to go."

"Dear Lord," I said, "don't send me there. Please. Just send me anywhere, but I don't want to go there. Besides that, this man is an older minister — he's old enough to be my daddy. I just don't want to go."

The more I prayed, the more the Lord said, "I want you to go."

Finally, I said, "All right. I'm going." So I went.

A young man and his wife who were graduates of a Bible college went with me to help me. The woman played the piano and her husband sang and led the congregational singing. They also sang special songs.

After I preached the first night at this pastor's church, this couple told me, "We wondered if you were going to teach on faith and healing, because we know this pastor and we know he doesn't understand biblical faith and healing." (The pastor used to be this woman's pastor.)

I had put it off as long as I could. Finally, I couldn't put it off any longer. I knew in my spirit what God wanted me to teach on. I announced that I'd be teaching the Bible along a certain line on a certain night.

Usually, this young man and his wife sat on the platform because the building was full, but that night they sat down on the front row. They told me afterwards, "We wanted to sit down front so we could see the pastor's face. He was sitting right behind you."

It's the most difficult thing in the world to preach faith

and have a pastor sitting on the platform in back of you breathing the hot breath of unbelief down your back. You don't even have to look back there; you can just feel it. That's tough sledding! But experiences like that in life do you good. They toughen you up.

Endure Hardness as a Good Soldier of Jesus Christ!

Paul said to Timothy, a young minister, "... *endure hardness* ..." (2 Tim. 2:3). Oh, it's easy enough to endure when everything is going good — when things are easy. You don't have to endure much then. As long as everything is going good, it's easy to endure and to maintain the glow. But Paul told Timothy, and this goes for every Christian, "... *endure hardness, as a good soldier of Jesus Christ.*"

Preaching when you can feel the pastor's hot breath of unbelief down your neck, is enduring hardness! That's when you really see if you can maintain the glow! I could feel that pastor's unbelief as he sat behind me. I didn't dare turn around to look at him. Actually, I could almost see the pastor's reactions on the faces of those in the congregation, because they were watching their pastor, and I could almost read every one of *his* reactions by how *they* reacted!

Endure hardness as a good soldier of the Lord Jesus Christ! I just kept plowing for about forty minutes. I just kept on going. Finally, after about forty minutes, the pastor sitting behind me came alive. Suddenly he burst out and said, "Amen!" and he jumped up. "Amen!" he said, "Folks, Brother Hagin is right. Bless God, what Brother Hagin is teaching is right! He's right!"

This wasn't the only time I had to preach or teach under these kinds of circumstances; it seemed like this happened to me a lot back there before people understood biblical faith and healing. Do you think that was easy? No! But you've got to maintain the glow in spite of the circumstances, because circumstances won't always be pleasant. Sometimes God will require you to do things that may be tough sledding for a while.

I remember another experience along this same line. Again, the pastor who had invited me to preach in his church was old enough to be my daddy. He was a leader in his particular denomination, and he had announced to his congregation some time before I got there, "The very idea of ministers calling people out and telling them what's wrong with them! The very idea of telling people that they've got a hernia or a rupture, or something else wrong with them! Don't they know God doesn't heal like that?" (Of course, he was talking about ministering by the gifts of the Spirit.)

Although this pastor had invited me to hold a meeting in his church, I knew he didn't understand certain biblical principles of faith and healing. I knew when I started preaching I would be plowing his field crossways, but I also knew the Lord had sent me there, so I just kept plowing. I just kept teaching and plowing.

One night there was an older gentleman in the congregation whom the pastor had said was the finest Christian he'd ever known. This older gentleman was more than eighty years old. The pastor himself was in his fifties, and he'd been pastoring for about thirty-five years, so to say that this older gentleman was the finest Christian he'd ever known was quite a statement.

That night I just pointed to this older gentleman. (I didn't know him personally, except that the pastor had briefly introduced me to him.) I said to him, "The Lord shows me you have a double hernia. You've been operated on twice and it came back on you again, and now you have a double rupture. If I'm wrong, just say so."

"No," he said, "you're right."

"The Lord told me to tell you to come down here," I said, "and that when I lay hands on you, both ruptures will disappear instantly." He came down to the altar, I laid hands on him, and both ruptures disappeared instantly.

You see, the pastor didn't understand this kind of ministry; he had told his congregation that God wouldn't heal people this way. The next night, however, he got up and announced to his congregation, "Folks, listen. I want you to hear me. I've been wrong. What Brother Hagin is teaching and the way he is ministering is right. What he's teaching about faith and healing is right! If he calls you out, just come on down to the front. And if he calls me out, I'll come down here too!"

But you think that was easy? No! But you've got to maintain the glow regardless of circumstances. You've got to maintain the glow regardless of what people say about you. You've got to be fervent in the Spirit in season and out of season — whether you feel like it or not!

If you'll be fervent in spirit no matter what happens, no matter what the circumstances of life are, you'll have a song in your heart and you'll be able to maintain the glow of the Holy Spirit in spite of difficult situations.

Chapter 8
Second Characteristic of Those With a Fresh Anointing

Let's look at a second characteristic of one who is constantly being filled with the Spirit.

Giving Thanks

EPHESIANS 5:20
20 GIVING THANKS always for all things unto God and the Father in the name of our Lord Jesus Christ.

Does the Bible admonish us to give thanks for a few things? To give thanks if it suits us? No, we are told to give thanks for all things!

This doesn't mean that we are to thank God for what the devil is doing. But in the midst of every circumstance, no matter what it is, we can thank God for His goodness. We can thank God that we have another opportunity to believe Him and trust Him. We can thank God that we have another opportunity to exercise our faith and to see His faithfulness and righteousness performed on our behalf.

Those Christians who are full of the Spirit are also full of thanksgiving and praise. They are full of song; they sing and make melody in their hearts to the Lord, and they are full of thanksgiving and praise to God.

Nowhere in the Bible do I find that God tells Christians to grumble, gripe, complain, and fuss. No! He tells them to give thanks.

"Yes, but no one ever recognizes me in the church! No

one thinks I'm important." Thank God for it! "Yes, but no one ever asks me to sing a special song." Thank God for it! "No one ever asks me to serve as an usher." Thank God for it! Give thanks to God for all things! That means in every circumstance maintain a heart that is full of thanksgiving and praise to God.

Too many times folks want to be seen and heard by others. That's their motive for wanting to do things in the church — they want to be noticed. They want to sing, so folks will notice them. Maybe they can't even sing! You ought to thank God no one asked you! If you're not qualified to sing, you're liable to get embarrassed and embarrass everyone else too.

No one ever asks me to sing either. Of course, if anyone ever heard me sing, you'd understand why! I don't sing unless everyone else is singing and then I just do what the Bible says, I make a joyful noise! I even took voice lessons at one time, but the voice teacher said to me, "I've been teaching voice for 39 years. I never told this to anyone else, but if I were you, I believe I'd quit trying to learn to sing." That's about the only thing you'll ever hear me say I can't do. I just can't sing, but I can have a song in my heart and make melody unto the Lord.

"No one ever asks me to do anything!" Thank God for it! No matter what happens, maintain a thankful attitude. I'm going to praise God regardless of circumstances.

I've said for a good many years that if someone told a lie about me, I wouldn't even take time to deny it. I'd just say, "Praise the Lord!" and go on down the road praising and worshipping God. I'm not going to let anyone or anything steal my joy. I just refuse to do it!

And I'm going to praise God whether I feel like it or

not. The Bible talks about offering up the *sacrifice* of praise — that's part of the function of a priest and as we saw, we're all called to be priests unto our God. One thing about it, if you stay filled with the Holy Ghost, it's the easiest thing in the world to offer up a sacrifice of praise to God. Praising God becomes just automatic; it becomes a lifestyle.

If you're full of praise and thanksgiving, you're full just like a sponge when it's full of water. You press that sponge anywhere, and water comes out. It's full! Just squeeze it the least bit and water comes out. If you're full of thanksgiving, no matter what happens, thanksgiving comes out. I don't care how much pressure the devil puts on you to try to squeeze you, thanksgiving comes out. That comes with maintaining a fresh anointing in your life — *be being* filled with the Spirit.

Praising God Puts the Devil To Flight!

When you are born again and baptized with the Holy Spirit and you're continually praising God, that brings the anointing and puts the devil on the run! Satan won't hang around where people are praising God. The devil can't stand that!

I remember a church we pastored during World War II. There was a young man in the congregation who recounted the following story:

This young man was going to Bible college to prepare for the ministry. In the summertime he would go out and preach so he would have enough money to pay his tuition in the fall. Then in the fall he would return to Bible school. One fall he was traveling back to the Bible college by bus.

The bus was crowded — it was so full of people that there was only standing room.

The bus was running late, and this young man had to make a connection and transfer to another bus. If he missed that connection, there wouldn't be another bus he could take for quite some time.

As the crowded bus he was on was approaching the bus terminal, this young man thought to himself, *Oh, dear Lord, this bus is going to pull in and the other bus is going to pull out before I have time to get off and transfer.* He was sitting toward the back of the bus where it was crowded and many of the people were swearing and telling vulgar jokes. Also, many people were standing up blocking the aisles, making a quick exit almost impossible.

About that time the young man saw the other bus pull into the bus station. He was the only one who had to get off at that particular stop, and he had to make a quick exit, but too many people were blocking his exit. Although he didn't mean to do it, amidst all this swearing and vulgar talk, without thinking he said out loud, "Praise the Lord! Thank God I'm saved!" He thought to himself, *Dear Lord, Did I say that out loud?*

Immediately, everyone stopped talking and looked at him. Then very quickly everyone backed out of his way! That whole crowd just parted and stood back and let him get off the bus! He marched down the aisle and as he began to get off the bus, he thought to himself, *Well, I've already done it anyway! I might just as well do it up right!* So as he was stepping off the bus, he said loudly, "Hallelujah, glory to God! I'm glad I'm saved!" and went out the door unhindered and transferred to the other bus before it pulled away!

That crowd reacted just like the devil does when we praise God! Once you begin praising God, the devil will shut up, step back, and get out of your way! When this young man praised God, those people on that bus didn't have anything else to say! The devil won't either because he doesn't like to hear Christians praising God!

I sometimes tell the story about an incident that happened to Rev. John Osteen and me. I was preaching in Houston, Texas, and Brother Osteen came to my meetings. After one of the meetings, Brother Osteen asked me to go to lunch with him and to stop by one of the local auto dealerships so he could finalize a deal on a car.

We went into this dealership and there was one automobile in particular that Brother Osteen was interested in buying. As we walked up to look at it, the manager approached us and asked us if he could help us. Brother Osteen said, "Yes, I want to buy this car," and he handed the manager a business card with the name of a salesman on it who had quoted him a price on that particular car.

The manager looked at that figure and started swearing. He said, "We can't sell you this car at this price!" Brother Osteen told him that was the price he had been quoted by the salesman, and he'd come to buy that car!

The manager let out another long string of curses. This manager was a tall man, but Brother Osteen who's not so tall, got right up in his face and began saying, "Glory! Hallelujah! Praise God! Glory to God! Praise the Lord!"

As soon as Brother Osteen did that the manager immediately stopped swearing. Brother Osteen said, "I demand equal time! If you're going to curse Him, I'm going to praise Him!" That manager instantly changed the way he was talking and acting! After that, you'd have thought he was the most religious person in town. (Incidentally, Brother Osteen bought that car for the price that was originally quoted him!)

The devil can't stand it when we praise God either! Every one of us is anointed to pray and to praise God. If you don't feel anointed when you start praying, stay in the Presence of God long enough and wait for the anointing to come. If you will offer the *sacrifice* of praise, that is, if you will praise God even when you don't feel like it, the anointing will come.

A Lifestyle of Praise

P. C. "Dad" Nelson made a great impression on my life. One reason he did was because of his Baptist background. I was born and raised Baptist. Dad Nelson had been in the ministry for 32 years as a Baptist and had 12 years of higher education. At that time, he was one of the most educated men in the world. I personally heard him say that he could read and write 32 different languages. Linguistics, or languages was his major in college.

I heard Dad Nelson give this testimony. He said one of his college seminary roommates was a pastor of a First Baptist church, and he invited Dad Nelson to come and preach for him. He got there just in time for the morning service. Dad Nelson said, "Sitting there on the platform, I said without thinking, 'Praise God!'" He had just recently been baptized with the Holy Spirit. He had been born of the Spirit before, but he'd just recently been baptized with the Holy Spirit. When Dad Nelson said, "Praise God!" his former roommate jumped and looked at him, because they didn't do that in the First Baptist Church.

I could relate to that because for the first 17 years of my life, I went to a First Baptist church, and I never heard anyone say "Praise the Lord!" or "Glory to God!" in a service. There was a time or two that some of the older men sitting over in the corner sounded like they grunted. Momma said one of them said, "Amen" one time.

Anyway, Dad Nelson said, "I thought nothing about it. Several different times I praised God out loud." Then he was introduced and came to the podium and preached his sermon. After the service, he and his seminary friend went out to eat. As they were sitting there waiting for their order to come, every so often without thinking, Dad Nelson said, "Praise the Lord!" or "Glory to God!" or "Hallelujah!"

Finally, his friend spoke up and said, "I believe that's just a habit with you." Dad Nelson said, "What do you mean?" He didn't even know what the fellow was talking about. He wasn't conscious of the fact that he'd said anything. You see, when you get full of the Holy Spirit, giving thanks is such a way of life to you, that you are unconscious of the fact that you are doing it. It's so much a part of you, that praise and thanksgiving just come out as a natural expression to God.

Dad Nelson asked his seminary friend, "What's just a habit with me?" "Well, praising God all the time like you do. I believe that's just a habit with you." "Well," Dad Nelson answered, "it's a habit I never used to have before I got filled with the Holy Spirit!"

Dad Nelson not only got filled with the Holy Spirit, he maintained a constant experience of staying filled with the Holy Spirit! That's why the praises of God were continually flowing out of his mouth!

When you get anointed with fresh oil, praise and thanksgiving will continually flow out of your mouth to God. If you've had a hard time praising God because of the tests and trials you're going through at the time, if you begin to praise and thank God you'll get your joy and your praise back! You'll get your thanksgiving back! Praise and thanksgiving will begin to roll out of your mouth once again. You'll be full of thanksgiving and joy.

When this seminary friend saw that praise and thanksgiving was a lifestyle with Dad Nelson, it changed his thinking. Although he was the pastor of a First Baptist church, he got filled with the Holy Spirit and spoke with other tongues. Evidently he liked that habit so well, he wanted to have it too!

Chapter 9
Third Characteristic of Those With a Fresh Anointing

We've already looked at two of the three outstanding characteristics of *be being* filled with the Spirit as mentioned in Ephesians 5:18-21: *Speaking* to yourself supernaturally in tongues and in psalms, hymns, and spiritual songs; singing and making melody in your heart to the Lord; and *giving thanks* continually unto God.

Submitting to One Another

The third characteristic we will look at in this chapter is *submitting* to one another in the fear of the Lord. This is where true submission comes in. We are to submit ourselves to one another in love as unto the Lord.

One of the characteristics the Bible lists of being filled with the Holy Spirit is being willing to submit to one another: *"Submitting yourselves one to another in the fear of God"* (Eph. 5:21). What does the Bible mean by, "Submit yourselves to one another"? This is a passage of Scripture some folks take out of its context and try to make it say something it isn't saying. Is the Bible referring to this extreme submission teaching we've all heard preached? Emphatically, no!

To submit means to give in to one another. It doesn't mean that you rule over one another, certainly not. But it means that you give in to one another and that you're not hardheaded and stubborn and always demanding your own way. It's the opposite of the attitude, *"I'm going to have my own way no matter what!"* or *"I've got my say-so and I'm going to have it!*" If you get saved and filled with the Holy Spirit, you'll overcome that attitude. You won't be so interested in having your say-so anymore!

Most Christians believe in submitting one hundred percent as long as it's others who are doing the submitting *to them.* But when it comes time for them to submit to someone else, that's another story. Then all of a sudden, they don't believe in submission anymore!

Believers who are filled to overflowing with the Holy Spirit have a submissive spirit or attitude toward others. That is, they don't find it hard to submit or give in to one another in an attitude of love. They don't always have to be right and to have the last word, so to speak. They are so *filled* with the Spirit of God that they don't demand their own rights and their own way. They want what God wants, and God's way is always love — putting the other person first.

You see, when you're *filled* with the Holy Spirit, you have a submissive spirit and you don't always need to have your own way. Submitting means giving in to one another in a spirit of love and meekness. There are some times when it might be better if you *didn't* have your say-so! Sometimes it might be better to just keep your mouth shut and not say anything, even if you do have the right to have something to say in the matter.

Submission indicates a broken and a humble spirit. Christians are to learn to submit to one another in the fear of God. It's easy when you're *filled* with the Spirit to submit to the other fellow in the fear of God. Also, when you're filled with the Spirit and you're maintaining the glow of the Holy Spirit, you're not hard to get along with.

Now notice the next verse.

EPHESIANS 5:22
22 Wives, submit yourselves unto your own husbands, as
unto the Lord.

Some people take that verse out of its context too, and
read it: "Now wives, you do what you're told to do, or
else!" However, the word "submit" in this verse is the
same word that's used in the previous verse telling fellow
believers to submit to one another in an attitude of love.

As we said, to submit means to give in to one another
and not always needing to have the last word about everything, and it is certainly *not* ruling over one another. Therefore, when the Bible talks about submission in the
marriage relationship, it is not talking about the husband
ruling over his wife with an iron fist, so to speak, any more
than it's talking about believers ruling over one another.
Biblical submission is referring to Christians getting along
with one another by submitting to each other in love. We
are to maintain a teachable, humble spirit, and walk in love
toward one another.

Therefore, we can readily see that a characteristic of
being filled with the Spirit is that you are willing to submit or to give in to one another in an attitude of love.

The Danger of a Know-It-All Attitude

Every one of us needs to be teachable and humble, and
to submit to one another in love. I've said for years that
I wouldn't listen to any teacher who wasn't willing to be
taught. All of us need to maintain a teachable spirit. I'm
always willing to learn. A know-it-all spirit or attitude is
contrary to biblical teaching.

A know-it-all attitude says, "I'm right and everyone else is wrong. You can't tell me anything because I know it all, and *I'll* tell *you* a thing or two!" For a Christian to have an attitude like that is dangerous! With an attitude like that you're liable to wind up dying prematurely because God may just have something He wants to get across to you through someone else in the Body of Christ.

I recall an experience I had along this line with a certain pastor. The pastor had already invited me to come and hold a meeting in his church, and the Lord told me He wanted me to go.

"But, Lord," I said, "I don't want to go to that church."

The Lord said, "I want you to go."

"Why do You want me to go there?"

The Lord replied, "Because that pastor is going to die unless he judges himself, and he's only 43 years old. He's not old enough to die. But if he'll get in on your morning teaching classes, and listen to My Word and put it into practice, he won't die — he'll live."

So at this pastor's invitation I came to his church to hold a meeting for him. Although I was a guest in his church holding a meeting for him, do you know he didn't come to *one* meeting! He was too busy! He was busy all the time.

We can be too busy! By the same token, we can also be so busy that we don't have time to listen to others and we become unteachable. This pastor was *too* busy. He had a daily radio program and he was building a new church. He had invited me to come and hold this meeting for him, but he never came to one of his own services! Not one!

Finally, his wife said to me, "Brother Hagin, talk to

my husband. See if you can get him to come to the day services," she said. Think about that! A pastor's wife having to ask a traveling teacher to talk to the pastor to try to get him to come to his own meetings! I wasn't there putting on my own meetings. I was a guest speaker, holding meetings for him.

I kept after him to come to the meetings, but he was always too busy. Finally, we got over into the third week of the meetings, and I asked the pastor's wife, "Why do you want me to get him to come to these services?" I wanted to find out what she knew, because the Lord had already told me he was going to die prematurely if he didn't change. There were some adjustments he needed to make, and if he didn't make them he would die prematurely, although that wasn't God's will.

The pastor's wife said to me, "Brother Hagin, I want him to go to the morning services because I know he's going to die if he doesn't change."

"How do you know he is going to die?" I asked. "He's only 43 years old. He's not old enough to die."

"I can't tell you how I know," she said. "I just know it on the inside. I just have an inward conviction that he's going to die."

Then I told her what the Lord had told me.

"That's right!" she said. "I know that's true, and I know it doesn't have to happen. We're both ordained ministers but through the years, we would never listen to anyone else. We thought we knew just as much as anyone, and we would never listen to anyone else."

That's not a submissive attitude, is it? That's not submitting one to another or having a teachable spirit. It's impossible to be fervent in spirit and to maintain the glow of the Holy Spirit if you don't have a humble and a teachable spirit.

"Talk to him," she asked me. "Ask him to come to the services."

I did talk to him again, but it didn't do any good. Finally, it was the Wednesday of the third week of the meeting. We only had two more day services and then the meetings would be over. We'd already had thirteen services — thirteen hours of teaching that he'd missed on the subject of faith and healing.

After the morning service we went out to eat — the pastor, his wife, and I. We were sitting in the restaurant eating, and I began to talk to him. I thought, *If I can just get him into these last two services, maybe he can get enough of the Word in him so that he'll correct himself. After all, it's not God's will for a person to die prematurely.*

This was Wednesday at noon, and we were going to close the meeting that coming Sunday night. I had already announced to the congregation that I would be leaving after the Sunday night service. I was going to start another meeting Tuesday night in a city a hundred miles away.

Finally, sitting in that restaurant with that pastor and his wife, in desperation I just blurted out, "Did you know you're going to die? You're only 43 years old. You're not old enough to die!"

"I know it," he said. "I know I'm going to die."

"How do you know it?"

"I just have an inward witness about it," he said.

Every believer has an inward witness.

"The Lord told me that you're going to die," I said, "but that you don't have to die. That's why He wanted me to come here and hold this meeting in your church. He said that you were going to die, but that you didn't have to if you'd come and listen to the Word and put the Word into practice in your life and make the necessary changes the Lord is requiring of you."

You know what that pastor said to me? I'm talking about not having a teachable spirit! He said, "Brother Hagin, I know God led me to ask you to come and hold these meetings in my church. I wanted my people to hear you, and I know what you're teaching is right. My wife's coming every day and she tells me what you teach in the services. I know what you're teaching is right. But, you see, if I came to the services, I'd have to admit that I'm wrong and you're right, and I'd rather just go ahead and die than to admit I'm wrong."

When that pastor said that to me — it was just like someone standing behind me was talking — the Lord said, "He'll fall dead in his pulpit one week from this Sunday night." And, you know, he did just exactly that. He fell dead in his pulpit one week from that Sunday night.

Why did that happen? Was that God's best? No, but that pastor wasn't teachable! He wouldn't receive what the Lord had for him and he wouldn't make the necessary adjustments in his life. He didn't have a submissive, teachable spirit. You ask, "Was he lost? Did he die and go to hell?" No, thank God, he made heaven. But he missed God's best for his life.

I want God's best, don't you? I'm not satisfied with second best.

Maintain a Teachable Spirit

A teachable spirit is a submissive spirit. I'm willing

to be taught, aren't you? I'm not talking about being taught someone's *ideas* or someone's *opinions.* I'm not going to just accept someone's idea that can't be proven by the Word of God. I don't mean some farfetched notion that someone dreamed up by taking some isolated text out of its setting and out of its context to try to prove some ridiculous theory. You can take verses of Scripture out of their context and make the Bible say anything you want it to say. I'm not talking about that.

But if someone brings me light and revelation from the Word of God, I'll receive it, and I'll be ready to walk in the light of God's Word! But you know someone doesn't have a teachable spirit when you bring the Word of God to them, and they get offended — and I mean to people who have been saved and filled with the Holy Ghost!

Christians ought to have a teachable spirit. By not having a teachable spirit, we can miss many blessings that God has for us.

I remember just such an incident when I could have missed a valuable spiritual truth God wanted to get over to me if I had not stayed open and teachable. I was in a service listening to a certain minister speak, and I could tell right away that he wasn't accurate in his understanding and teaching of certain scriptural truths. Also, in his teaching he made a derogatory remark about the so-called "faith" message which showed that he really didn't understand Bible faith. I could have gotten offended at his ignorance of the Word of God and closed my mind and shut him off right there. But I just stayed open and gave him the benefit of the doubt and said to myself, *He probably didn't mean that quite the way he said it.*

Keeping an open mind and giving others the benefit

of the doubt is part of maintaining a teachable spirit. We can miss many blessings God intends for us by getting offended and shutting our minds to what others have to say. For example, in this particular instance, there had been a spiritual question that I'd been wrestling with for probably twenty years or more. But after this minister made that derogatory remark, it wasn't more than five or ten minutes later that the Holy Ghost answered that question for me through this very minister.

I thought to myself afterwards, *What if I'd closed my mind to what he was saying? What if I had just shut him off? I still wouldn't know the answer!* If I had gotten offended and shut my mind off to this minister and had not remained teachable, God wouldn't have been able to use him to get that spiritual truth across to me; I wouldn't have been open to receive anything from him. But because I stayed teachable, even though he didn't think quite like I did or maybe didn't have as much light in certain areas as I did, God was able to bring me light on this subject I'd been wrestling with through him. I've said for years, and it bears repeating — you can disagree without being disagreeable.

Disagree Without Being Disagreeable!

When I was a young pastor, it was customary in churches in those days to have a revival in the local church every three months whether or not you needed it, and whether or not God had directed you to do it. This was just the way they did things back then in the local church. So we had a revival every three months in our church. During the revival we always had a guest speaker come in and hold meetings for at least two weeks and sometimes longer. Then in another three months, we would begin another revival.

So every year we'd have at least four revivals in our church. Special speakers would come in to minister or to preach, and sometimes others would come in and preach just on the weekend. You can readily see that over a period of a year quite a few guest speakers held meetings in my church. Out of all those speakers, I never did agree one hundred percent with any of them. We agreed on the basic doctrines of the Bible, of course; they preached the gospel of the Lord Jesus Christ just as I did. But I did not agree one hundred percent on every little thing any of them said. Not a single one of them! But just because I didn't agree with *everything* these guest speakers preached in my pulpit, I didn't just jump up in the middle of the service and say, "Now you're all wrong about that! Let me straighten you out!"

In fact, during the entire twelve years I pastored, there was one particular minister with whom I disagreed the most, and yet we had more people saved and filled with the Holy Spirit in his revivals than in any other revival in the church!

Also, I grew enough spiritually in a year or two so that I began to agree with some of these other ministers; I saw that they were right and I was wrong. But some of them I never did agree with, and some I still don't agree with. But that doesn't mean that they weren't good Christians or godly ministers of the gospel just because they didn't believe everything just like I did. But again, we can disagree without being disagreeable!

I'm not talking about pastors allowing other ministers

to preach gross error in their pulpits without correcting doctrinal error. That would be contrary to the Bible, because the Bible says that we are to hold fast to sound doctrine (Titus 1:9; 2:1; 1 Thess. 5:21). I'm talking about disagreeing on minor issues. We're not all going to agree on every little thing, but we can disagree and still be agreeable and walk in love and maintain a teachable spirit toward one another!

After all, if God had to wait until we were all perfect in every aspect of our lives and completely mature in our spiritual growth and knowledge of the Word before He could use us, He wouldn't be able to use *any* of us! But I've always taken great comfort and encouragement from the Scriptures that tell us God used a donkey to arrest Balaam and get his attention (Num. 22:21-35). Surely if He could use a donkey, He can use me — or anyone else in the Body of Christ for that matter!

Maintain a teachable spirit. It will help you maintain the glow of the Spirit in your life! There is no way you can be filled with the Spirit without maintaining a teachable spirit in your life.

Submit to Scriptural Correction

There's another area where we need to maintain a teachable, submissive spirit. I've had people come to me wanting to tell me their "revelation." I've told them, "I'll listen to your revelation, but we'll have to judge it in the light of God's Word. Also, the Word of God teaches, *'Let the prophets speak two or three, and let the other judge'*" (1 Cor. 14:29).

Some of these people didn't have a teachable spirit;

they didn't want their revelation judged. The unteachable people who came to me would never allow their revelation to be judged. Some of them told me, "I'm not going to have *my* revelation judged!"

I've said to those unteachable people, "Forget it then. You ought to get full of the Holy Spirit, and then you'd be willing to submit your revelation to be judged in the light of God's Word."

"No! I'm not going to have my revelation judged! I'm just as full of the Holy Spirit as you are, and I'll whip you to prove it!"

Yes, I've had people offer to whip me to prove they're just as filled with the Holy Spirit as I am! They claimed they were full of the Holy Spirit! I'm not in favor of being filled with that kind of spirit. That's the wrong spirit; that's a devilish spirit.

No, when people have the right spirit, they don't mind the least bit in the world being corrected. It's true that we need to be careful to correct people in the right way — in a spirit of love and gentleness. But we are to submit to one another in the fear of God and not be unteachable with one another! The Bible also says, "Prove all things," and that "all things should be done decently and in order" (1 Thess. 5:21; 1 Cor. 14:40). If people have the right spirit, they aren't afraid to have their revelation judged by the scrutiny of God's Word.

Decently and in Order

Speaking of doing things decently and in order, I think Rev. and Mrs. J. R. Goodwin had the best order in their church in Pasadena, Texas, of any church I was ever in.

Brother Goodwin has gone to be with the Lord now, but he was a fine pastor and teacher. When I went to Brother and Sister Goodwin's church to preach, Brother Goodwin would tell me, "If some of our people feel that they have something from the Lord such as a message in tongues and interpretation, prophecy, or word of knowledge, they'll lift their hand. When you're in the pulpit and you want to recognize them, that's fine. If you don't wish to recognize them, that's fine too. It won't bother them the least bit in the world. I've taught them to be teachable and to submit to spiritual authority."

You see, Brother Goodwin had taught his people to have a teachable, submissive attitude. I also believe Brother and Sister Goodwin's church was the most Spirit-filled church I've ever seen. That goes right along with what Paul said in Ephesians 5:18,21: "Be filled with the Spirit . . . submitting yourselves. . . ." When you're constantly being filled with the Spirit — when you maintain a fresh anointing of the Holy Spirit upon your life — you have a submissive, humble spirit.

In talking about proper order in a church, Paul said, *"Let all things be done decently and in order"* (1 Cor. 14:40). If you stop and analyze that, Paul said this in connection with the operation of spiritual gifts in the church. Well, if he said operating the gifts of the Spirit can be done *in order,* that means they can also be operated in a way that is *not* in order.

That's why Brother Goodwin had said to me, "If you want to recognize those who feel they have something from the Lord when you're teaching in the pulpit, fine. But if you don't recognize them, they won't be offended." They had humble, submissive spirits; they were teachable and they recognized spiritual authority.

You see, if the person who is in charge of the meeting is inspired by the Holy Spirit, it stands to reason that the Holy Spirit won't interrupt Himself. Sometimes folks would lift their hand when I was teaching in Brother Goodwin's church, and I knew they evidently had something, but then on the other hand, since I was in charge of that particular service, I already had something in my own spirit. I knew exactly what the Holy Spirit wanted to do in that service.

You see, God is not going to hide from the one who is in charge of the service what He wants to do. But if everyone is just jumping up and doing one thing and then another, you'd have the most chaotic disorder you've ever seen. However, there are different kinds of services, and this would be more appropriate at a believers' meeting. (For more information about the different kinds of meetings, *see* Rev. Kenneth E. Hagin's book, *Plans, Purposes, and Pursuits*.)

But you can see how important it is to maintain a humble, teachable attitude and to stay filled up with the Holy Spirit. And from the characteristics listed in Ephesians 5:18-21, it's evident who is filled to overflowing with the Spirit, isn't it? When you're filled with the Spirit, you have a song in your heart and you're continually giving thanks to God. You have a submissive, teachable spirit, and you maintain unity with one another. That pleases God!

In that kind of atmosphere is it any wonder that when the early Christians prayed in Acts 4:31, the place where they were assembled together was shaken and they were all refilled with the Holy Ghost! How many of them received a fresh anointing? All of them! *"They were all filled with the Holy Ghost, and they spake the word of God with boldness."*

What did those Christians do to receive a fresh anointing? Did they gripe, fuss, and complain? No, they prayed together in one accord, and they spoke to themselves in psalms, hymns, and spiritual songs. They were continually singing and making melody in their hearts to the Lord. If you're griping, fussing, or complaining, you need a fresh anointing! If you're not submitting one to another, if you get angry when others don't recognize you, or you always have to be right — you need a fresh anointing!

Dead Formalism or a Fresh Anointing?

ECCLESIASTES 10:1
1   Dead flies cause the OINTMENT of the apothecary to send forth a stinking savour....

Notice the word "ointment." That comes from a Latin word meaning *to anoint.* The margin of my King James Bible has a footnote by the words "dead flies." It says, "Flies of death."

Before we were born again, we were in spiritual death — that is, we were separated from God. But after we were born again, we were delivered out of spiritual death and translated into the Kingdom of God's dear Son, the Lord Jesus Christ. We shouldn't allow back into the church the cold, dead formalism that was in the church when we were still in spiritual death — when we were dead in our sins and trespasses before we were born again.

That's where the problem lies in the church today!

There's too much dead formalism in the church, and it produces a stinking ointment instead of a fresh anointing. Dead formalism is robbing the church of the *anointing!* No, we need to look to the New Testament to find God's pattern for everything we do so we won't be a "stinking ointment"! If we follow God's pattern for being continually filled with the Holy Spirit, a fresh anointing will abide upon us and we'll be full reservoirs to God's glory!

If you're filled with the Spirit and you maintain that fresh anointing, there will be a song in your heart! Not "dead flies" — not a stinking savor — but a song! A fresh anointing, not a stinking ointment! If there's a song in your heart, it'll show up on the outside. It'll show up on your face. You won't have to notify your face if you're happy; it'll just show up on your countenance!

Continue to stay filled with the Spirit! Speak to yourself in psalms, hymns, and spiritual songs. Stay in God's Presence long enough so there is a continual flow from your heart to the Lord! If you're filled with a fresh anointing of the Holy Spirit, thanksgiving and a singing heart will be a lifestyle with you and you'll have a submissive and teachable spirit. You'll have a fresh anointing on your life from God, not a stinking ointment!

Smith Wigglesworth once said, "I'd rather have a church full of people who didn't have the baptism of the Holy Spirit and all of them hungry for God, than to have a church full of people that had received the baptism of the Holy Spirit and had lost their hunger for the things of God." People with no hunger for God remind me of that verse in Ecclesiastes 10:1: "Dead flies in the apothecary send forth a stinking savour." Spiritually speaking, a person can stink.

Every single one of us needs a fresh anointing! Stay in God's Presence until you are anointed from on High. Speak to yourself in psalms, hymns, and spiritual songs; sing and make melody unto the Lord! Declare, "I shall be anointed with fresh oil! Thank You, Lord, for the fresh anointing! I receive it now!"

Chapter 10
A Fresh Anointing Is Recognizable

You see, spiritual health is just as obvious as physical health. You know when people aren't feeling well, don't you? It shows up in the way they look and act. Did you know that spiritual health is the same way? It is just as obvious whether or not someone is in good spiritual health; it's recognizable. It's recognizable when someone is so filled up with the Spirit that they radiate the glow of the Holy Spirit.

It must be recognizable because we read in Romans 12:11 where the Bible said, "Be fervent in spirit," or "Maintain the glow." If it wasn't recognizable, you wouldn't know whether you were maintaining the glow or not. Also, when the Bible said, "Be filled with the Spirit." If it's not recognizable, you wouldn't know whether a person was filled with the Spirit or not.

I remember years ago I read a message by one of the pioneers of the Pentecostal movement, and he made mention of the fact that some years before he had been the pastor of a church. He had asked a missionary who was returning to the U.S. to speak in his church.

In those days people traveled primarily by train. This pastor went to the train station to meet the returning missionary. As soon as the missionary saw the pastor, he discerned right away that spiritually something was wrong with the pastor. One of the first things he asked the pastor was, "What's the matter?"

The pastor replied, "Nothing's wrong."

"Yes, there is," the missionary said. "Something is the matter. You're not where you ought to be spiritually;

you're not up to par."

"Nothing's wrong," the pastor insisted.

The pastor later related, "I drove the missionary back to the parsonage, and by the time we got there, God had begun to deal with me that I had not been truthful with him. So later that evening I went to his room to tell him the truth. I knocked on his bedroom door, and he invited me to come into the room. I said, 'You said to me earlier that I'm not where I should be spiritually. You said that something was the matter with my spiritual health. I said there wasn't anything wrong with me spiritually, but I've repented for saying that because there is. I must tell you the truth.' "

The pastor lived and pastored his church in quite a large city. He said to the missionary, "For a number of years, in fact, when you left our city last, my church was the only Full Gospel or Pentecostal church in this city. But since then another man moved to this city (he wouldn't even call him 'brother') and started a church across town. He came in on *my* territory to start a church!"

Surprised, the missionary said to the pastor, "But there are several hundred thousand people in this city!"

The pastor replied, "Actually there's even more than that now because the city has grown since you were here last. I imagine now there are about one million people or so in the metropolitan area of this city."

The missionary looked at the pastor, and somewhat taken aback, said, "Do you mean to tell me that you've been upset because someone else came and started another church in this city! You ought to be glad! Do you mean to tell me that you actually lost out with God and lost the glow in your spiritual life because you had something against another minister? You ought to be glad God sent another minister to this city! You ought to pray that other ministers would come and start churches in this city!''

This pastor had lost out with God because he let a little something get into his heart against another person. It showed up in his countenance; in his spirit. It was recognizable. This pastor's spiritual "health" and well-being was almost the first thing the missionary noticed when he saw him; the missionary saw immediately that the pastor wasn't where he ought to be spiritually.

The pastor later related, "I knew what the missionary said was right. So before our church even started the first service with that missionary, I got in my car and went across town and apologized to this other pastor. I said to him, 'Come and fellowship with us. Let's start another church here in this city.' "

Once he made it right with this other pastor, they both began to maintain the glow! And the blessings of God fell upon them mightily.

Spiritual health is discernible. That missionary discerned right away that spiritually there was something wrong with that pastor. First of all, he didn't have that glow or that *fervency of Spirit* the Bible talks about. A Christian can't maintain the glow of the Spirit if he's holding a grudge against another person.

Because this pastor had something in his heart against someone else he was no longer a full reservoir. Remember Jeremiah 2:13: Broken cisterns can hold no water. Unforgiveness and holding grudges will cause the vessel to break and leak! This pastor had become an empty cistern because he had something in his heart against another man of God so there was no way he could maintain the glow or be fervent in Spirit! His heart wasn't right with God. Spiritual health is discernible!

Filled and Running Over

Being filled with the Spirit is recognizable! When you are filled with the Spirit, your cup is filled and running over!

> **PSALM 23:1-6**
> 1 The Lord is my shepherd; I shall not want.
> 2 He maketh me to lie down in green pastures: he leadeth me beside the still waters.
> 3 He restoreth my soul: he leadeth me in the paths of righteousness for his name's sake.
> 4 Yea, though I walk through the valley of the shadow of death, I will fear no evil: for thou art with me; thy rod and thy staff they comfort me.
> 5 Thou preparest a table before me in the presence of mine enemies: thou ANOINTEST my head with OIL; my cup RUNNETH OVER.
> 6 Surely goodness and mercy shall follow me all the days of my life: and I will dwell in the house of the Lord for ever.

Many of the Psalms are prophetic and many of them are Messianic, that is, they are really prophesying about the coming Messiah, the Lord Jesus Christ. For example, if you'll read Psalm 22, you'll see that psalm is actually a picture of the crucifixion of Jesus. Notice Psalm 22:1 says: *"My God, my God, why hast thou forsaken me?...."* That's exactly what Jesus cried out on the Cross (Matt. 27:46). Psalm 22 was fulfilled when Jesus died and rose from the dead.

We are now living in Psalm 23. Jesus is the Good Shepherd. Jesus Himself declared, "I am the Good

Shepherd" (John 10:11). Notice Psalm 23 didn't say, "The Lord is my Shepherd; I am *full* of want"! It said, *"The Lord is my shepherd; I SHALL NOT WANT."*

Psalm 23 gives us a picture of God's anointed ones being anointed with fresh oil. Remember that Psalm 23 belongs to us. If it doesn't, let's just quit quoting it and leave it alone. If Psalm 23 doesn't belong to us, we might just as well tear that page out of the Bible and quit reading it. Too many people quote this psalm as just a beautiful something to recite. But, no, there's more to it than that.

We're living in Psalm 23 right now because the Lord *is* our Shepherd now; He's our *present-tense* Shepherd. He anoints our heads with oil. Our cup runneth over. Is your cup only half full? If it is, get a fresh anointing so your cup will run over! "He anoints my head with oil and my cup is running over!"

When you're filled with the Spirit and your cup is running over, you've got a bold, overflowing testimony. "My cup runneth over!"

Holy Ghost Boldness Is Recognizable

The disciples had boldness in their lives because they were so filled with the Spirit that their "cups were running over." In chapter 4, the disciples were taken into question because the lame man at the Gate Beautiful was healed. We've looked at these scriptures before to see the biblical pattern of numerous refillings of the Holy Spirit, but let's look at them again to see the boldness of the disciples.

ACTS 4:1-13
1 And as they spake unto the people, the priests, and the

captain of the temple, and the Sadducees, came upon them,

2   Being grieved that they taught the people, and preached through Jesus the resurrection from the dead.

3   And they laid hands on them, and put them in hold unto the next day: for it was now eventide.

4   Howbeit many of them which heard the word believed; and the number of the men was about five thousand.

5   And it came to pass on the morrow, that their rulers, and elders, and scribes,

6   And Annas the high priest, and Caiaphas, and John, and Alexander, and as many as were of the kindred of the high priest, were gathered together at Jerusalem.

7   And when they had set them in the midst, they asked, By what power, or by what name, have ye done this?

8   Then Peter, FILLED WITH THE HOLY GHOST, said unto them, Ye rulers of the people, and elders of Israel,

9   If we this day be examined of the good deed done to the impotent man, by what means he is made whole;

10 Be it known unto you all, and to all the people of Israel, that by the name of Jesus Christ of Nazareth, whom ye crucified, whom God raised from the dead, even by him doth this man stand here before you whole.

11 This is the stone which was set at nought of you builders which is become the head of the corner.

12 Neither is there salvation in any other: for there is none other name under heaven given among men, whereby we must be saved.

13 Now when they saw the BOLDNESS of Peter and John, and perceived that they were unlearned and ignorant men, they marvelled; and they took knowledge of them, that they had been with Jesus.

The disciples demonstrated boldness because they were filled with the Spirit of God. The Word of God tells us very plainly that Peter and John were ignorant and unlearned men. What was recognizable among the people was *not* how much theology and psychology the disciples knew, but that the disciples had knowledge of *Jesus.* They didn't know a thing in the world about theology, but they knew Jesus, the Word of God made flesh (John 1:14). There's nothing wrong with education, but what makes the difference is knowing Jesus! Paul, for example, was a learned and an educated man. But Paul said, "I count all that as dung for the knowledge of Christ" (Phil. 3:8). Paul had a revelation of Jesus.

The disciples knew the Word! They had the Holy Spirit! And that makes all the difference in the world. They knew *the Word and the Holy Ghost.* If you get away from the Word and the Holy Ghost you've gone too far for me. But I believe that the Word will work for us and the Holy Ghost will move now just as in the days of the apostles and the Early Church.

Because the disciples were filled with the Holy Spirit, they had boldness: "... *when they saw the boldness of Peter and John* ..." (Acts 4:13). Being filled with the Holy Ghost is what gave them their bold, overflowing testimony! They maintained the spiritual glow of the Holy Spirit by being so filled up with the Spirit that a bold testimony was a lifestyle with them. If you stay filled with the Spirit, you will have a bold testimony too! "He anoints my head with oil, and my cup is running over."

However, a bold testimony brings persecution. We read that the disciples suffered persecution for their bold testimony. They were taken by the priests and elders of the people and taken into questioning. But persecution keeps the fire burning.

ACTS 4:23,24,29-31
23 And being let go, they went TO THEIR OWN

COMPANY, and reported all that the chief priests and elders had said unto them.
24 And when they heard that, they lifted up their voice to God with one accord, and said, Lord, thou art God, which hast made heaven, and earth, and the sea, and all that in them is. . . .
29 And now, Lord, behold their threatenings: and grant unto thy servants, THAT WITH ALL BOLDNESS they may speak thy word,
30 By stretching forth thine hand to heal; and that signs and wonders may be done by the name of thy holy child Jesus.
31 And when they had prayed, the place was shaken where they were assembled together; and they were all FILLED with the Holy Ghost and they spake the word of God with BOLDNESS.

Notice how the disciples prayed in verse 29: ". . . *grant unto thy servants, that with all boldness they may speak thy word.*" It's good to pray for boldness. Christians need to do that. I think most of us need to pray that we would be more bold. The disciples prayed for boldness and look at the results in verse 31: "*And when they had prayed, the place was shaken where they were assembled together; and they were all filled with the Holy Ghost, and they spake the word of God with boldness.*"

Friends, too many times the supernatural power of God is waning among us. The Bible says that we should, ". . . *earnestly contend for the faith which was once delivered unto the saints*" (Jude 3). We need to contend for the faith with all boldness! The supernatural should be natural with God's people. If we would contend for the faith, the supernatural would be natural with God's people.

How can we keep a bold testimony? By constantly

being filled with the Spirit. Do we want to be empty cisterns or full reservoirs. Which one are you? You can receive a fresh anointing and be a full reservoir!

Being filled with the Spirit is recognizable! The people recognized the disciples had been with Jesus and were full of the Holy Ghost because they spoke the Word with boldness! If you've lost your boldness, you need a fresh anointing! A fresh anointing brings with it a bold, overflowing testimony.

Manifestations of the Supernatural

When you're filled with the Holy Ghost, there will be manifestations of the supernatural power of God in your life. Of course, we realize that manifestations of God's power operate as the Lord wills, not as we will.

Because the disciples were filled with God's power, the supernatural power of God was demonstrated in their midst.

ACTS 13:6-12
6 And when they [Paul and Barnabas] had gone through the isle unto Paphos, they found a certain sorcerer, a false prophet, a Jew, whose name was Bar-jesus:
7 Which was with the deputy of the country, Sergius Paulus, a prudent man; who called for Barnabas and Saul, and desired to hear the word of God.
8 But Elymas the sorcerer (for so is his name by interpretation) withstood them, seeking to turn away the deputy from the faith.
9 Then Saul, (who also is called Paul,) FILLED WITH THE HOLY GHOST, set his eyes on him,
10 And said, O full of all subtilty and all mischief, thou child of the devil, thou enemy of all righteousness, wilt thou

not cease to pervert the right ways of the Lord?
11 And now, behold, THE HAND OF THE LORD is upon
thee, and thou shalt be blind, not seeing the sun for a
season. And immediately there fell on him a mist and a
darkness; and he went about seeking some to lead him by
the hand.
12 Then the deputy, when he saw what was done, believed,
being astonished at the doctrine of the Lord.

Some people have erroneously said that God struck
Elymas the sorcerer with blindness (v. 11). No, God didn't
strike Elymas with sickness or disease. The Bible says the
hand of the Lord came upon him, and he was blind for a
season. But Elymas was not blind with sickness or disease.
The supernatural power of God came upon him and
rendered him blind for a season!

You see, because the disciples were filled with the Holy
Spirit, the supernatural power of God operated through
them, not as they willed, but as the Spirit willed. If you
want the supernatural power of God to manifest through
your life as the Spirit wills, you'll have to stay filled up
with the Holy Spirit too. Of course, you will have to live
a life of obedience to God. And you can't just sit around
and wait for God *to make* you do something — to make
you get filled with the Spirit or to make you get filled up
with His Word. He's not going to *make* you do anything.
But if you want the supernatural power of God operating
in your life, stay filled up!

Extremes in the Church Today

There are some basic problems or extremes in the
Church today when it comes to the supernatural move of

God and the manifestations of the Holy Spirit and gifts of the Spirit. Some folks just don't believe in any supernatural manifestations of God's power at all. And some folks have seen such excesses and fanaticism even in Full Gospel, Pentecostal circles, that they're in the ditch on one side of the road and they don't *want* the supernatural move of God's Spirit.

Then other folks have gotten way over in a ditch on the other side. They desperately wanted God to use them and they were full of zeal, but they lacked wisdom. And because they wanted God to use them but they weren't full of the Word of God and wisdom, they got into the ditch on the other side and got into error by trying to perform in the flesh.

Let's just do what the Bible says to do! Let's stay full of the Word of God. Let's be sure the Word of God dwells in us richly *in all wisdom.* And let's be full of the Spirit of God. The Word first; then the Holy Spirit. And in everything we do whether it is in *word* or in *deed,* let it glorify the Lord. He is the One we want to be lifted up and glorified.

Chapter 11
Full of the Word and the Holy Spirit!

Christians who are filled up with the Word of God and the Holy Spirit are easy to recognize. Acts chapter 6 tells us that being filled with the Spirit and being full of the Word is recognizable.

ACTS 6:1-6
1   And in those days, when the number of the disciples was multiplied, there arose a murmuring of the Grecians against the Hebrews, because their widows were neglected in the daily ministration.
2   Then the twelve called the multitude of the disciples unto them, and said, It is not reason that we should leave the word of God, and serve tables.
3   Wherefore, brethren, look ye out among you seven men of HONEST REPORT, FULL OF THE HOLY GHOST [the Spirit] and WISDOM [the Word], whom we may appoint over this business.
4   But we will give ourselves continually to prayer, and to the ministry of the word.
5   And the saying pleased the whole multitude: and they chose Stephen, a man FULL of faith and of THE HOLY GHOST, and Philip, and Prochorus, and Nicanor, and Timon, and Parmenas, and Nicolas a proselyte of Antioch:
6   Whom they set before the apostles: and when they had prayed, they laid their hands on them.

The twelve apostles were the only ministers the Church had at that time. The disciples said, *"It is not reason that we should leave the word of God, and serve tables"* (v. 2). Therefore, seven men were selected and appointed to serve tables. Evidently these were the first deacons. The Greek word translated "deacon" means *helper* and these men were elected to help the disciples so the disciples could give

109

themselves more fully to the study and preaching of the Word.

Many times in the church today when church leaders select others to fill certain positions or offices, they just focus on whether the candidates for the position are filled with the Holy Spirit or whether they *were* filled with the Spirit at one time. They forget about the fact that they need to be people of honest report and they need to have a reputation for being full of wisdom or full of the Word of God.

Remember the verse we read in Colossians 3:16: *"Let the word of Christ dwell in you richly in all wisdom. . . ."* The Bible says that even those who are chosen to the deacon's office, not only need to be full of the Spirit of God and wisdom, but they must be of honest report. Deacons often take care of finances in a ministry; they often handle church finances. You don't want people with a dishonest report handling your money. No, you want someone who is of honest report, full of the Holy Ghost, and full of wisdom. People can be full of the Holy Ghost, but lack wisdom in some areas.

Therefore, in selecting people for church offices, we need to choose people who have all three of these qualifications: Men and women of *honest report, full* of the *Holy Spirit,* and *full* of *wisdom.* One or two of these qualities is not enough! We need Christians who possess all of these qualities if we're going to operate according to the Bible.

The Bible tells us in verse 3 that an honest report is recognizable. For one thing, if an honest report weren't recognizable, the disciples wouldn't have known which men to select for this position!

You know yourself, you could say about a person, "I

don't know whether we ought to put him in a position of authority or not. For one thing, he owes everyone in town — he doesn't even pay his debts. Besides that he can't be trusted." People like that are not of honest report, are they?

On the other hand, someone who is reputable in every area is recognized by all. For example, you could say about a person, "His reputation in all matters is impeccable. He has a fine reputation in the community financially and in every other way. I'd trust him in any position in the church!" A man or woman's reputation follows him or her, and an honest report is recognized by all.

Also, being full of the Holy Ghost must be recognizable or how would the disciples have known whom to select? By the report that you get about people it is quite obvious whether or not they are honest and whether or not they stay full of the Holy Spirit and the Word of God. And as we've seen, spiritual health is recognizable.

Just as a side thought, notice Acts 6:6, where these men who were chosen to be the first deacons were brought before the disciples: *"Whom they set before the apostles: and when they had prayed, they laid their hands on them."* If it's important to lay hands on men and set them aside to serve as deacons, you can see how much more important it is to lay hands on those who are called into the full-time or fivefold ministry.

Let's look at an instance in the Bible where men were set apart for the fivefold ministry. I think we can glean something from this.

ACTS 13:1-3
1 Now there were in the church that was at Antioch

certain prophets and teachers; as Barnabas . . . Simeon . . .
Lucius . . . Manaen . . . and Saul.
2   As they ministered to the Lord, and fasted, the Holy
Ghost said, Separate me Barnabas and Saul for the work
whereunto I have called them.
3   And when they had fasted and prayed, and laid their
hands on them, they sent them away.

Notice the Bible said they prayed and then laid hands
on them. It didn't say, "They laid hands on them and then
prayed." They laid their hands on them and sent them
away — not broken cisterns but full reservoirs!

Don't Lose the Anointing!

I've been in the ministry for more than fifty years, so
I'm not just exactly a novice when it comes to the
ministry. Besides, in more than fifty years of ministry,
you wouldn't have to be too brilliant just to stumble over
a few things by accident and learn some things that way!
But I've observed this: pastors and other ministers can
get so involved in making money on the side, running
businesses and selling this product or that product, that
they can lose the anointing to preach.

I've known some ministers who had two or three
businesses on the side and were so involved running them
that they had no time to study and prepare for the
ministry. Then when they got up to preach, they were no
more anointed than last year's bird nest. And they
wondered why their preaching was dead and their churches had grown cold!

Some of these ministers had marvelous abilities to
preach and teach but they lost the anointing because they

were constantly taken up with business details. How sad when they could have really done something for God! Of course there are duties and responsibilities that pastors must attend to — the business of the church! But I'm talking about pastors whose time and attention gets entirely taken up with the business affairs of running the church or ministers who get so involved in running their own businesses on the side that they have no time for the Word of God or prayer.

If deacons are to be full of the Holy Ghost and wisdom, so should those who are called to the fivefold ministry! Over the years, I've seen some pastors quit the ministry just because they didn't use wisdom in the way they did some things. For example, I remember one pastor who had a congregation of 400 people, and sometimes for special services, 500 people. During special services when there were 500 people, there was standing room only, so he decided to build a 1,000-seat auditorium to accommodate his largest crowds.

I said to him, "If you're going to build an auditorium, build it in such a way that you can close off part of it. Otherwise, if you take 400 people and put them in a 1,000-seat auditorium, there will be 600 empty seats. That will cause the people to wonder where everyone is and get discouraged, when in reality the church congregation is just as large as it ever was. If your people get discouraged, and you can't fill up your sanctuary, you will get discouraged too and want to leave.

This particular pastor said to me, "Oh, but I'm going to take this city for Jesus!"

"How long have you been pastoring in this city?" I asked him.

"Oh, eight or ten years."

"Well," I said, "if you haven't taken the city in eight or ten years, it stands to reason it might take you a few more years to 'take the city.' If it took you eight years to go from 165 people to a congregation of 400 — then you'd do well to have 650 in another eight to ten years. And if you build a 1,000-seat auditorium, you'll still have 350 empty seats."

"Oh," he said, "but we're going to do it! We're going to win this city for Jesus in just eighteen months!"

I said, "Now I'm not talking unbelief, but I don't think you are. Use some wisdom. You've been here all this time and you haven't won the city yet. Don't misunderstand me, you're doing a good job, but you need to use some wisdom in your building project so you and your people don't get discouraged."

Well, he went ahead and built his 1,000-seat auditorium anyway. I preached a crusade for him in that big auditorium, and many of the seats were tied off with ropes. Of course, everyone sat down toward the front, so it looked like there weren't many people in attendance. Very shortly after that, he got discouraged and left the church.

It's fine to build a larger church than what is necessary for the present congregation; however, provision ought to be made in the construction of the building so part of the sanctuary can be partitioned off. That way it could be used for certain special occasions which draw larger crowds, but also certain parts of it could be closed off when it wasn't in use. That way the pastor won't get discouraged and neither will his people.

I saw pastor after pastor make that same mistake in their building projects. I tried to get them not to be unrealistic. I advised them, "Don't build huge auditoriums that are too large for your present congregations unless you can close off part of the auditorium. Otherwise, it will ultimately hinder your growth because the people will become discouraged from coming. For example, the typical Wednesday night crowd is usually smaller than the crowd on Sunday morning, and so when the people come on a Wednesday night to a 1,000-seat auditorium, they will wonder where everyone is."

Sad to say, within about eighteen months to two years, every one of these pastors I cautioned was gone — they left their churches. They got disillusioned because they weren't able to fill those big auditoriums right away, so they left. And their congregations were left with those big church buildings!

One Foursquare pastor was the only one I saw who used wisdom in his church building project. I held a meeting for him, and although his building could hold 750 people, on the other hand, his normal crowd was only about 250 people. But because of the way the building was constructed, 100 people in the main sanctuary on a Monday night looked really good. When the lights were off in the balcony, it was just naturally closed off, and under the balcony he had folding doors which could be shut. If he needed to use the rooms under the balcony, he could open the doors. He used those rooms for Sunday school classes, and he could open them up if he had to.

Our meeting started off on a Monday night, and I counted 99 people. It looked like we had a good crowd, because he had all those other rooms and the balcony closed off. But before the week was out he had to open up the folding doors underneath the balcony to accommo-

date all the people, and on some of the nights we even had
to open up the balcony. He used wisdom in his planning.

You can readily see that if the apostles were careful
to choose men who were full of wisdom to wait on tables
and take care of ministry business, then it must be important for pastors to be full of wisdom too. These men in
Acts chapter 6 were chosen for their wisdom!

There's something else I want you to see in this passage
of scripture.

> **ACTS 6:4,5**
> 4   But we will give ourselves CONTINUALLY to prayer,
> and to the ministry of the word.
> 5   And the saying pleased the whole multitude. . . .

The disciples gave themselves continually to prayer,
and to the ministry of the Word. Is it any wonder they
had a fresh anointing upon their lives and the supernatural
power of the Spirit of God was a normal part of their lives!

Just a side thought, it's interesting to note that the
preacher said something that pleased the whole crowd! The
reason the preacher could say something that pleased the
whole crowd is that they were all *filled* with the Holy
Spirit. They weren't half full; they weren't empty cisterns;
they were full reservoirs and they were all in one accord!
And we know this crowd included many disciples because
the Bible says, ". . . *the twelve called the multitude of the
disciples unto them* . . ." (Acts 6:2).

The Early Church had probably grown to at least 8,120
people by this time because we know that 120 people had
received the baptism of the Holy Spirit on the day of
Pentecost; 3,000 were added to the church when Peter

preached (Acts 2:41); and 5,000 were added to the church
when Peter and John preached after the man at the Gate
called Beautiful was healed (Acts 4:4). Therefore, we know
that the Early Church probably had at least 8,120 members at this time and probably more than that because the
Word says, "... *the Lord added to the church daily such
as should be saved*" (Acts 2:47).

We also know that the Church — those first converts —
hadn't left Jerusalem yet. The Early Church was still
gathered together in Jerusalem because we read in Acts
8:1 where the church was dispersed and scattered throughout Judaea and Samaria. But up until that time the
Christians were still in Jerusalem.

So here's a multitude of people — probably at least
8,120 — and the preacher said something that pleased the
whole multitude! Dear Lord, you could have 20 now and
not be able to say something that pleases the whole crowd!
Do you know why? Because they're not filled up with the
Spirit! They may have had that initial experience of being
filled with the Holy Ghost, but they have not had those
refillings — those *fresh anointings*. But if you get people
filled up to overflowing with the Holy Spirit, it makes all
the difference!

Also, what the disciples said pleased the multitude
because those early Christians were fervent in Spirit, and
they had a hunger for God. If people aren't hungry for God,
they're broken cisterns that are empty! Don't ever lose
your hunger for God. If you're hungry for God, you'll seek
many refillings of the Holy Spirit.

ACTS 6:5,8
5 And the saying pleased the whole multitude: and they

chose Stephen, a man FULL OF FAITH and of the HOLY GHOST, and Philip, and Prochorus, and Nicanor, and Timon, and Parmenas, and Nicolas a proselyte of Antioch. . . .

8   And Stephen, FULL OF FAITH AND POWER, did great wonders and miracles among the people.

There's that word "full" again! Stephen was full of faith and full of the Holy Ghost. The disciples chose someone who was *full* of faith and *full* of the Holy Ghost. If you're full of the Holy Ghost, you're full of power. But if you don't have any faith mixed with the power of God, all the power in the world won't do a bit of good!

Full of the Holy Ghost! That's why God was able to use Stephen to do great wonders and miracles among the people. Too many preachers are full of the wrong things. But stay full of the *Holy Ghost!* Get full of the *Word* and then what you'll talk about is the Word.

What Are You Full Of?

I held a revival for a certain pastor, and I was there for four full weeks. I ate at least the noon meal with him every day, and then sometimes after church we'd go out and have something to eat. So I ate with this pastor at least twice a day and sometimes three times a day for four weeks or about twenty-eight days.

Every single time we went to eat, he'd tell me at least three new jokes. He never repeated himself. Well, if I had eaten with him twice a day, that would be six new jokes a day he'd told me. If I'd eaten with him three times a day, that would be nine new jokes each day. Out of all those jokes, I can only remember *one!* Well, if you multiply six times twenty-eight, that's more than one hundred and fifty jokes that pastor told me while I was there holding this meeting for him.

In my meetings, I *quoted* most of my scriptures by heart. Once when we went out to eat, this pastor said to me, "I wish I could remember scriptures like you can." Finally, I said to him, "You know, if you'd feed on the Word like you do on jokes, you *could* remember scriptures. I can't remember jokes like you do because I'm not interested in jokes. That's why I can't remember them — I'm just not interested in them. I'm interested in the Word!" I don't know about you, but I like to stay full of the Word!

What are you full of? The Bible didn't say to be full of jokes or things that are insignificant and of little importance. The Bible said to be full of the Word! If you're full of the Word, then that's what you're going to talk about.

MALACHI 3:16
16 Then they that FEARED the Lord spake often one to another: and the Lord HEARKENED, and HEARD it....

Throughout the Old Testament we see that expression "to fear the Lord." That's not talking about being afraid of God like you'd be afraid of a tornado or a rattlesnake. That word carries with it the thought of a holy or reverent awe of the Lord! We are to reverence the Lord, and to have a holy awe for Him. If the Church wants the supernatural move of God's Spirit, we're going to have to get back to that holy reverence for God and the things of God.

Well, if the Lord heard those saints of God back then

in the Old Testament who reverenced Him, I wonder if
the Lord still hears us today? Or do you suppose He's
gotten so old He's lost His hearing! Maybe we should take
up an offering and get Him a hearing aid! No, thank God,
His hearing is not impaired. His hearing is just as good
as it always was!

> **MALACHI 3:16**
> 16 Then they that feared the Lord spake often one to
> another: and the Lord hearkened, and heard it, and a book
> of remembrance was written before him for them that
> feared the Lord, and that thought upon his name.

It says the Lord *hearkened* and *heard* what those who
feared the Lord said to one another. The word "hearken"
means *to listen to, to give attention to,* and *to give heed
to.* The Lord paid attention to what they were saying and
He *heard* what they were saying. I wonder if they were
telling jokes to one another? Is that what caused the Lord
to hearken and to hear them? No, they weren't full of jokes;
they were full of the Word! They were full reservoirs, not
empty cisterns. They had a reverential awe for His Name!

> **MALACHI 3:17**
> 17 And they shall be mine, saith the Lord of hosts, in that
> day when I make up my jewels; and I will spare them, as
> a man spareth his own son that serveth him.

Glory to God! Did you ever stop to think about it?
We're the Lord's jewels! There's a note in the margin of
my *King James Bible* and by the word "jewels," it says,
"special treasures." We are the Lord's special *treasures!*
The Bible says those who fear God and think upon His

Name are His special treasures. As the Lord's special treasures, let's stay full of His Word and full of His Spirit. Let's bring the Lord the honor and glory due His Name by being full reservoirs, not empty cisterns. Let's not be full of our own plans, and full of our own ways; let's be full of God's Word and full of His Spirit!

We as the Church of the Lord Jesus Christ need to take advantage of the provision God has given us to be full reservoirs! We can't do it apart from the anointing! It will take a fresh anointing for each of us to be full reservoirs, but this is what God intends for us. If we follow God's New Testament pattern for being continually filled with the Holy Spirit, a fresh anointing will abide upon us and we will be full reservoirs to God's glory. Stay in God's Presence and in His Word so you can say with the psalmist, "I shall be anointed with fresh oil"!